Dennis Budkowski,

Warm best wishes
for a Merry Christmas &
the best of New Years.

Carol Kowalski
12-8-81

THE IMPACT OF COLLEGE ON PERSISTING AND NONPERSISTING STUDENTS

THE IMPACT OF COLLEGE ON PERSISTING AND NONPERSISTING STUDENTS

Cash Kowalski

Philosophical Library
New York

Copyright, 1977, by Philosophical Library Inc.
15 East 40 Street, New York, New York 10016
All rights reserved

Library of Congress Catalog Card No. 76-14498

SBN 8022-2185-8

Manufactured in the United States of America

DEDICATED

To the memory of my father, Peter
and
my mother, Bernadine
wife, Luba
brother, John
sister, Irene,
uncle, Stanley, and
sons, Joseph, Matthew and Peter.

TABLE OF CONTENTS

List of Tables		ix
Foreword		
By Dr. Robert H. Shaffer and Dr. Raymond C. Gibson		xiii
Preface		
By Dr. Constantine W. Curris		xvii
Acknowledgments		xxi

Chapter

I. INTRODUCTION ... 1

  Background of the Research ... 1
  Methods and Procedures ... 7

II. REVIEW OF SELECTED RESEARCH AND LITERATURE ... 18

  Selection of College ... 19
  Characteristics of College Environments ... 19
  Characteristics of Persisting Students ... 21

	Characteristics of Nonpersisting Students	31
	Nonpersisting Students: Influence of Home Environmental Factors	32
	Nonpersisting Students: Influence of College Environmental Factors	33
	Nonpersisting Students: Influence of Personal and Academic Characteristics	35
III.	ANALYSIS OF DATA	50
	Comparative Data	50
	Home Environment	50
	College Environment	52
	Academic Factors	52
	Personal and Academic Factors	61
	Significant Chi-Squares	64
IV.	SUMMARY, CONCLUSIONS, RECOMMENDATIONS, EPILOGUE AND COMMENTS	72
	Summary of Background and Procedures	72
	Methods and Procedures	73
	Findings	74
	Conclusions	77
	Recommendations	77
	Epilogue	79
	Some Comments by Dr. Joseph P. Cangemi	81
	BIBLIOGRAPHY	85
	Appendix A: Definition of Terms	100
	Appendix B: Questionnaire	102

LIST OF TABLES

Table   Page

1. Descriptive Data of the 1973 Fall Semester Sample of Persisting and Nonpersisting Students of a Major Midwestern University   9

2. Similar Characteristics of High School and College Dropouts   40

3. Home Environmental Factors for Persisting and Nonpersisting Students   51

4. College Environment: A Comparison of Satisfaction With the Atmosphere and Living Conditions by Persisting and Nonpersisting Students   53

5. College Environment: A Comparison of the Needs to Talk With and Evaluation of the Attitude of the Academic Advisors and Faculty Members by Persisting and Nonpersisting Students — 54

6. College Environment: Use and Evaluation of the Student Personnel Services by Persisting and Nonpersisting Students — 55

7. Academic Characteristics: A Comparison of Educational Plans Upon Entering College Between Persisting and Nonpersisting Students — 56

8. Academic Characteristics: A Comparison Between Persisting and Nonpersisting Students — 57

9A. Personal Characteristics: A Comparison Between Persisting and Nonpersisting Students — 58

9B. Personal Characteristics: Use of Alcoholic Beverages and Nonprescription Drugs by Persisting and Nonpersisting Students — 59

10. Personal And Academic Characteristics: A Comparison of the Purposes of Higher Education and Their Practice At a Major Midwestern University As Perceived by Persisting and Nonpersisting Students — 61-62

11. Specific Reasons For Withdrawing From a Major Midwestern University by Nonpersisting Students — 63

12. Factors Influencing The Decision to Withdraw and Transfer by Nonpersisting Students — 64

13. Home Environment: Father's Education and Problems At Home — 65

14. College Environment: Satisfaction With Atmosphere And Evaluation of Attitudes — 66

15. College Environment: Student Personnel Service — 67

16. Academic Characteristics: Educational Program — 67

17. Academic Characteristics: Basic Skills, Study Habits And Interest, Class Participation And Attendance, And Library Use — 68

18. Personal Characteristics: Discouragement, Happiness And Parental Pressures — 70

19. Personal And Academic Characteristics: Career Plans, Becoming Well Rounded, Developing Judgment, And Learning Subject Area — 71

FOREWORD

TO PERSIST OR NOT TO PERSIST

Research regarding persisting and nonpersisting students has often been based on the explicitly stated or implicit assumption that persisting students are good and desirable and nonpersisting students represent failures. Such a posture is naive and selfseeking. Many institutions have studied the problem entirely from the point of view of increasing enrollment and maximizing tuition income. A student lost was thought to represent a certain amount of dollars, which, if he or she had been retained, would have automatically been put to an appropriate institutional use.

The topic as explored by Dr. Kowalski clearly is much more complex. From a student development point of view, persistence or nonpersistence must be related to the achievement of immediate and long-range personal goals and related to the motivation, skills, and progress of individual students as seen by themselves. Developmentally the student's self-image is as important in considering continued enrollment in a college or university as is the image of the student reflected by the institutional processes of grading and evaluation.

Students who "spend time" in a "hold" pattern merely waiting to grow up and enter the mainstream of adult life generally feel unfulfilled, immature and often as non-achievers, whereas many students have made a break with formal education and achieved maturity. Through heightened self awareness, formulation of life plans and development of realistic perceptions of themselves and the world around them they feel fulfilled and actualized even though they had dropped out of the formal system. Increasingly, current research is emphasizing the importance of perceiving formal and non-formal educational experience as an integral part of the total lifestream contributing to the development of the individual. In the future more individuals will enter and leave the formal educational world several times during their lives. The non-formal phase of their lives must be viewed as significant and utilized for the educational development of all individuals. College and university experience for all students ideally must contribute to such development.

When related to the individual development of students, the question of persistence and nonpersistence becomes one of fulfillment of clearly stated objectives, both near-term and long-term. This puts a new focus on counseling, financial aid and compensatory educational efforts.

Obviously, the economic question is an important one for most institutions. In such institutions admissions procedures and the questions of who should be recruited and admitted become significant. If, in fact, a place in the freshman class results in a net loss of dollars to the institution because a potential four-year graduating student was excluded by the admission of one who did not persist, then the data concerning such phenomena are clearly and properly significant areas of research. However, if the focus is upon who profits most from an educational experience, when do they profit most, and what can the institution do to assist students who profit most, the research focus might be slightly different.

Institutional goals, commitment and resources become significant and relevant topics of attention.

Some individuals need the beginning experience in a formal educational institution before they understand the problems they must face as they grow and develop. Further, they often learn by experience what the formal educational process has to contribute to their total growth and development.

Another major area of concern in researching persistence and nonpersistence is the expectations which students bring with them to an institution and the expectations which an institution has of the students it admits. Institutions that build up false expectations in their recruiting process and purport to select students carefully must regard nonpersisting students as their failures. Institutions which attempt to be all things to all people and then feel shocked at their dropouts often have only their own vaguely defined and poorly enunciated goals to blame.

To the extent that nonpersisting student represent unproductive expenditure of personal, institutional and societal resources, they represent needed and significant research targets. The conditions which foster persistence in appropriately selected and counseled students need analysis and elaboration. Based upon research to date it is apparent that each institution must look at itself and its environment at the same time it looks at its prospective and current students. Only in the complete institutional context can appropriate and effective steps be taken to increase the retention of the students in any specific institution.

In short, the present research has revealed that the problem of the college dropout is one of grave complexity and much broader than one of mere retention of an individual's enrollment in a particular institution of higher education.

Department of Higher Education	Robert H. Shaffer
Indiana University	Raymond C. Gibson

Preface

In the euphoria of the early sixties, this nation made programmatic commitments to salvage human talent. The War on Poverty was launched, civic rights consciousness was translated into action, and an impressive list of legislative and institutional programs heralded a major societal effort to identify and develop human talent. Higher education was directly involved in these efforts. Student recruiters, Upward Bound counselors, and financial aid officers shuffled from the campus to ghetto and hollow. An euphonic air permeated the academy. We had embarked on a moral crusade to salvage human talent and to develop that talent into productive citizens, if not scholars.

As with so many social movements, the tone of reform—and implicit guilt for having long delayed reform—resulted in supportive campus movement. Students were to be protected from capricious or unnecessary separation from the University community. Counseling centers flourished, advising programs were scrutinized, compensatory education under a rubric of titles gained campus prominence, and grading systems came under increased attack from those who saw a pernicious character in "D" and "F" grades. Many hailed the ascendancy of egalitarianism in higher education. Enhanced expectations prevailed.

The seventies has brought a new and not so refreshing look at educational egalitarianism. Campuses are disturbed by reports that large graduating classes experience employment difficulties. Faculty committees are troubled by grade inflation problems and the implicit prostitution of the academic enterprise. A groundswell of faculty concerns about the academic preparedness of entering students—and even graduates—is influencing educational decision makers. Significantly, a money crisis in a period of serious inflation has brought new perspectives to state capitals, governing boards, and even campuses.

Many of the glamour programs of the sixties have become the whipping boys of the seventies. Bureaucrats and budget committees now view with a jaundiced eye many of the student life programs and policies so triumphantly inaugurated only a few years back. Open admission policies are being scuttled and a renewed emphasis to channel discretionary dollars into "pure" academic programs is present.

In these times empirical data are sorely needed to justify the continuation, and even expansion, of many educational services. Salvaging human talent is not an educational by-product but an educational mission. Our successes in this endeavor may be severely limited unless a sound and tenable rationale for funding this mission can be affirmed.

Dr. Kowalski's study is an excellent contribution to this rationale. The identification of factors distinguishing between persisting and nonpersisting students is critical if our limited resources are to be effectively employed in the attraction and retention of capable students. A concentration of these resources, rather than the frequent pattern of resource dispersal, may prove invaluable in fulfilling the challenge of salvaging human talent.

While Dr. Kowalski's research has considerable applicability to the work of faculty and student development personnel, one wishes that decision makers in both educational and bureaucratic institutions would carefully consider the findings, which he has persuasively presented.

        Constantine W. Curris
        President
        Murray State University

ACKNOWLEDGMENTS

I recognize that many personalities have helped to shape my academic life, and this publication does indeed reflect those influences; some I should like to mention.

The writer is indebted to Dr. Raymond C. Gibson and Dr. Robert H. Shaffer of Indiana University, who provided the writer with a meaningful educational experience through their kindness, encouragement, understanding and wisdom, and to Dr. Emmett Burkeen of Western Kentucky University who has encouraged and assisted the author in his professional achievements.

The author wishes to acknowledge a special note of thanks to Dr. Joseph P. Cangemi, of Western Kentucky University, who as an esteemed colleague and most of all as a friend, has always significantly helped the author on numerous occasions. Also appreciated was the computer expertise of Mr. Thomas Kesler of Indiana University and Dr. Lee Epstein's commentary. For contributions of a different nature the writer is indebted to his parents, wife, brother, sister, uncle and several close friends—Gene, John and Steve.

Special support and consideration was extended the author by the College Foundation of Henderson Community College, Henderson, Kentucky. The author is grateful for their support.

The work reflects essentially some of the best influences upon my life.

Chapter I

INTRODUCTION

Background of the Research

The school dropout problem is a national concern at all levels of education. Since the founding of Harvard in 1636, institutions of higher education have been confronted with the dilemma of students withdrawing from college, either voluntarily or because of influence and motivation from the administration.

The school dropout problem is not a new phenomenon; it is probably just one day, or several hours, younger than the schools themselves. A paper entitled "The Early Withdrawal of Pupils from School: Its Causes and Its Remedies" was presented to the annual convention of the National Education Association as early as 1872.[1]

The college dropout problem is an international problem. In Costa Rica, each student is interviewed by a social worker before withdrawing from school. This is one of Costa Rica's major educational research areas. In Great Britain, only the best students are admitted into colleges, and 75 percent of these receive government aid. Still 20 percent fail to graduate. The cost of this failure to the British economy is about $20 million a year ($1,200 per student, per year.)[2] The institutions in France use very selective admission procedures for entrance into college. Still they are confronted with approximately a 70 to 75 percent dropout rate.[3]

Historically, considerations were largely viewed from the standpoint of ignorance and the personal loss experienced by the dropout. Today, however, the problems related to the college dropout have become a loss to the university, loss of educated manpower to society,[4] and worst of all, personal failure with which the dropout is forced to live.

However, it is true that in recent years it has come to be recognized that dropping out may not be as serious a matter as it was once considered since many students may come back or reenter some other institution. In fact, some authorities recommend increased flexibility to provide for what are referred to as "drop-ins" and "drop-outs."[5]

In post-World War II era, it was extremely important for an individual pursuing a college degree to complete that degree within a four year period. This can partially be explained by the greater demand and the numerous opportunities in America's job market for college graduates at that time. Because of today's economic and social conditions, the completion of a degree in four years is no longer a definite indicator of success.[6]

In 1971, about 34 percent of all 2 year college students and 12 percent of all students enrolled in the first 2 years of 4 year colleges were attending part time.[7] For many students full-time college enrollment is not easily realized. There are a number of extraneous factors which help to explain this phenomenon. Some of these factors are personal, family obligations, and lack of finances.

Approximately 80 percent of all high school seniors in the United States hope to pursue post-secondary education. Over 60 percent of the graduating high school population enroll in some institution of higher education. Approximately 50 percent of high school seniors set their goals for college degrees.[8] In reality, not nearly all those who aspire to a college degree end up earning one. The illustration below reflects a cross sampling from college to college in those graduating on schedule:[9]

University of Georgia	35%
University of Iowa	37%
University of Wisconsin	38%
Pennsylvania State University	43%
City University of New York	45%
Hollins College	53%
Princeton University	80%

A review of the literature indicated that the average retention of the nation's colleges and universities of each 100 entering students is as follows: approximately 40 complete a bachelor's degree within four years, another 20 graduate in succeeding years, and approximately 40 fail to graduate at all. The studies by Laird, Pervin and Iffert also support these findings.[10] In addition to these data, numerous studies support a considerably higher attrition rate, approximately 50-60 percent.[11]

President Lyndon B. Johnson in 1965 expressed concern when he stated that 60 percent of the 10th grade students from poverty neighborhoods of our 15 largest cities drop out before finishing high school. The cost of this withdrawal runs high both for youth and the Nation.[12]

Data at the national level indicated a variety of reasons why students drop out of college.[13] Students leave for academic,[14] personal,[15] environmental,[16] financial,[17] emotional or psychological reasons.[18]

According to such researchers as Chickering, Berdie and Cope, significant differences were found in the characteristics of college students and the colleges themselves.[19] Feldman and Newcomb[20] have determined that general information is useful and beneficial for general purposes to assess students and their potentials. The specific problems of a specific school are not the same as the general indices developed from a plethora of studies.

Also, each college and university should be considered as a unique entity. The factors leading to students dropping out may well be unique to any given institution.

The major Midwestern university where the research was to be conducted was concerned about the withdrawal problem among its students. This concern was expressed in a written memorandum to the Chancellor's Office by the Office of Records and Admissions. The analysis by class standing reported the largest withdrawal at the sophomore level, followed by juniors. Freshman, senior and graduate withawals have remained relatively constant.[21]

Significance of the Research

The primary goal of an institution of higher education is to assist each person in fully developing his potential.[22] Every student is a unique individual and needs to be recognized as such. The concern for disciplines must yield to a concern for persons.[23] Institutions of higher education must be concerned with teaching men how to make a living and how to live.[24] The current needs and interests of individual students are the most significant factors that must be onsidered in developing programs of campus life.[25]

Institutions of higher education must continue to explore the problems confronting college withdrawals. Far too much talent is wasted when students abandon their educational goals and fail to arm themselves with the necessary learning that takes place over a period of time at an institution of higher education. Further, significant research points out that those with college degrees enjoy a better life financially and socially.[26]

It was reported that only 10 percent of the students who depart from college prior to earning a degree have some specific occupational preparation. Furthermore, this wastage is occurring at a time when the nation's economy needs more educated and skilled manpower. The Labor Department forecasted the employment situation for the 1970's and estimated that the demand for white collar workers will increase by about 50 percent.[27]

Lawrence A. Pervin stated that, "Colleges have a responsibility to their dropouts: to help make sure that dropping out becomes a profitable rather than a traumatic experience for the student." He further stated that this involves the college's interest in the individual's situation and in his future.[28]

One method of dealing with the college dropout problem is to study the college persisters. By investigating the characteristics of college persisters, valuable data can be gained which will better orient and educate students so that they will not withdraw prior to graduation. Another approach to decelerating the number of students withdrawing from college is to study the behavioral characteristics of the nonpersisters.

Statement of Problem

The problem of this research was to examine the differences between the home environments, college environments, and the personal and academic characteristics of persisting and nonpersisting students at the major Midwestern university where the research was to be undertaken. The population of this research was comprised of students enrolled during the fall, 1973 semester.

Within the design of this study three separate clusters of factors were examined. These factors were as follows:

1. The home environment as expressed by family size, parents' marital status, education of parents, and problems and pressures at home has an influence on persisting in college.
2. The college environment as expressed by the student's relationship with other students, his advisor, faculty mem-

bers, and the student personnel services has an influence on persisting in college.
3. The individual's personal, emotional and academic characteristics as expressed by his feelings of happiness-unhappiness, encouraged-discouraged, healthy-unhealthy, good study habits-poor study habits, self-confident—lacking self-confidence, adequate ability-inadequate ability, certain goals-uncertain goals, etc., have an influence on persisting in college.

Purpose of the Research

It appeared that little additional specific information regarding the factors affecting withdrawal at the major Midwestern university was available and thus, other research concerned with the dropout problem at the university was needed.

Assuming that the atmosphere at the Midwestern university is different to some degree from other universities, and further assuming that the students at this university are a unique group, then additional information may be needed about the specific characteristics associated with students withdrawing from this university. The present research attempted to contribute information relevant to the understanding of the variety of factors associated with the attrition of students from this large Midwestern university. Specifically, the present research examined the following: the home environment, college environment, and the student's personal, emotional and academic characteristics.

The information from this research may well be utilized to strengthen and improve existing programs or to create new programs to assist students with problems which may influence their decision regarding withdrawal from colleges and universities.

Null Hypotheses

The following null hypotheses, utilized for this research, were tested:

1. There is no significant difference between home environmental factors of persisting and nonpersisting students at a major Midwestern university where the research was undertaken.
2. There is no significant difference between college environmental factors of persisting and nonpersisting students at a major Midwestern university.
3. There is no significant difference between the personal, emotional and academic characteristics of persisting and nonpersisting students at the university.

Methods and Procedures

As previously identified, college students persist or withdraw from college for a variety of reasons. Very little specific and up-to-date information was available about nonpersisting students at this major Midwestern university. General information about persisting and nonpersisting students could have been obtained by interviewing faculty members, student personnel service workers, and by reviewing existing research and literature. However, such information would have been general and would not have generated an adequate body of specific data. Thus, a need existed to obtain additional in-depth information regarding characteristics of persisting and nonpersisting students at this university.

It was believed that the most accurate data could be obtained by directly asking students at the university about information pertaining to personal backgrounds, experiences, interests, goals, expectations, and feelings which could be associated with students persisting or withdrawing at this university. Therefore, a survey form of research was selected which allowed for the personal expression by the persisting and nonpersisting students of responses to a variety of items regarding their home environment, college environment, personal and academic characteristics.

Many criticisms have been leveled regarding mailed questionnaires and other self-reporting devices. Despite the limitations described in some of these criticisms, some of which appear to be valid, mail out questionnaires, introspective analyses, and self-reports still marshal useful data. Some of these data are intuitive, introspective and irrational. This condition probably should be expected since the behavior and/or attitudes being sampled are intuitive, introspective and irrational. Students' decisions to leave school frequently are impulsive and irrational. Students' decisions to stay in school, on the other hand, also often may be impulsive, intuitive, introspective and irrational.

Many of the influences surveyed in this research involved questions of values and estimates of aspirations. While some of these influences may possess factual bases, the interpretation based on the influential factors involved a question of value systems. Some of those value systems have been developed as a consequence of exposure to the environments being explored. The questionnaire may then be predictive as well as sampling effectiveness.

Overview of the Research

The general procedure in this research involved selecting two random samples of students from the large university where the research was being conducted. One sample was composed of persisting students and the other sample consisted of nonpersisting students. Further, the design called for the development of a questionnaire which allowed the students to respond to selected items related to the problems of college attendance. Questionnaires were mailed to a sample of persisting students and to a sample of nonpersisting students. This information was compiled into statistical data which, when analyzed, allowed for comparisons between persisting and nonpersisting students on selected factors.

In order to obtain a more accurate description of the persisting and nonpersisting students in this research, the following information was obtained from the Records and Admissions Office. The descriptive data are presented in the Table 1.

TABLE 1. DESCRIPTIVE DATA OF THE 1973 FALL SEMESTER SAMPLE OF PERSISTING AND NONPERSISTING STUDENTS OF INDIANA UNIVERSITY

Class/Sex	Persisting *N = 201				Nonpersisting *N = 165			
	N in sample	N of returns	$\bar{X}$ age	$\bar{X}$ gpa	N in sample	N of returns	$\bar{X}$ age	$\bar{X}$ gpa
Freshman								
Male	25	22	19.6	3.10	25	16	19.6	2.25
Female	25	23	19.0	3.26	25	23	20.0	2.71
Sophomore								
Male	25	18	20.5	3.20	25	16	21.8	2.26
Female	25	24	19.8	3.20	25	19	22.5	2.53
Junior								
Male	25	18	22.3	2.98	25	12	23.7	2.38
Female	25	25	21.1	2.99	25	17	22.5	2.79
Senior								
Male	25	15	23.5	3.08	25	11	23.7	2.60
Female	25	19	22.2	3.33	25	17	22.1	2.63
Graduate								
Male	25	18	24.3	3.29	25	20	28.3	2.95
Female	25	19	24.0	3.69	25	12	28.1	2.86

*N = number, $\bar{X}$ = mean, gpa = grade point average

The names and addresses of the persisting and nonpersisting students were randomly selected by computer. After the samples were selected, questionnaires were mailed to students in both groups. Information from the questionnaires was transferred onto addition, telephone calls were utilized to remind many of the local non-respondents. In order to establish credibility, a cutoff level for return of the questionnaires of 80 percent for the persisting students and 65 percent for the nonpersisting students was established *a priori*. The cutoff levels used in this study are based upon the percentage suggested by a research authority.[30] Of the 250 persisting students surveyed, 201 (80.4%) responded by completing and returning the questionnaire. Of the 250 nonpersisting students surveyed, 165 (66%) responded.

Questionnaire Validity and Reliability

Inherently, the questionnaire possesses face validity. Face validity addresses itself to the issue of questionnaire appearance. Each item in the questionnaire dealt with some aspect of the student's persistence in college or his failure to continue in college. No attempt was made to disguise items. Therefore, the questionnaire contains face validity.

Furthermore, nothing in the content of the questionnaire suggested offensive, threatening, or incriminating self-disclosure by the respondents. Therefore, the researcher assumed the respondents would not purposely have reasons to falsify their responses. A cover letter which was enclosed with the questionnaire explained the purpose of the study, explained that respondents need not identify themselves, assured the student that all information would be confidential, and stated that the individual information would be compiled into group data which hopefully could be used to help students at this large Midwestern university. The material in the cover letter further established a basis for assuming that subjects would respond honestly and accurately.

The questionnaire also possessed content validity. Content validity is the degree to which the sample of items in the questionnaire represents the content that the questionnaire is designed to measure.[31] Because the questionnaire was designed as a result of the review of literature and attempted to collect data on factors related to persisting or nonpersisting students, it was assumed that the questionnaire was sufficiently comprehensive.

A degree of reliability was established by consulting with a panel of judges and faculty members in construction of the pilot study questionnaire as well as with the construction of the final questionnaire. The questionnaire was field tested with several groups of students at a major Midwestern university. A pilot study surveyed persisting and nonpersisting students from this university utilizing the pilot questionnaire. The information from the pilot study was analyzed and from this analysis it appeared that the questionnaire items were concise, clear, and not vague, thereby enhancing the degree to which students would consistently respond.

Sample Selection

The sample consisted of 250 students randomly selected by a computer from the population of persisting students and 250 nonpersisting students randomly selected from the population of nonpersisting students. This information was summarized in Table 1.

A computer print out listing descriptive information (names, addresses, class, sex, age and grade point average) about the students was received from the university Records and Admissions Office.

On April 19, 1974, the appropriate questionnaire, cover letter, and self-addressed, stamped envelope were mailed to the 250 persisting students and 250 nonpersisting students. A copy of the questionnaire and cover letter used in the study are located in Appendix A.

On April 26, 1974, approximately one week after the questionnaires were mailed, a postcard was mailed to each of the nonrespondents requesting them to complete their questionnaire. The reminder was mailed to all subjects, both persisting and nonpersisting students, except those who had already returned the questionnaire. The names of the nonrespondents were easily identified because each questionnaire was discretely coded for follow-up purposes and for matching of descriptive data provided by the Records and Admissions Office. In the event any of the nonrespondents received the postcard and had already completed and mailed their questionnaire, they were asked to disregard the reminder.

The data from the returned questionnaires were analyzed at the computer facility of the Chemistry Department. A frequency distribution program was written in order to provide a listing of single column distribution of frequency counts and percentages for both groups.

Chi-squares were also completed for the various characteristics at the Wrubel Computing Center. The same program was also used to interpret significant chi-square values for factors identified at .05 level of significance.

REFERENCES

[1]Schreiber, Daniel, "700,000 Dropouts," *American Education*, 6:6, June, 1968.

[2]Pervin, L. A., *et. al.*, "The Dropout In Conflict With Society," pp. 3-21, in *The College Dropout And The Utilization Of Talent*, 1966, p. 12.

[3]Tournoux, J. R., *Le Mois De Mai Du General*, p. 49

[4]Vaizey, John, "The Costs of Wastage," *Universities Quarterly*, 25:139, Spring, 1971; Langlois, Eleanor, "*Graduate Attrition At Berkeley*," ERIC, no. ED 069 220, August, 1972, p. 1.

[5]Blaine, G. B., *et. al.*, *Emotional Problems of The Student*, p. vii, 98; Brown, R. D., *Student Development in Tomorrow's Higher Education—A Return to the Academy*, p. 18; *Less Time More Options—Education Beyond the High School*, pp. 1, 15 and 19.

[6]Gustavus, W. T., "Successful Students, Readmitted Students, And Dropouts: A Comparative Study of Student Attrition," *Social Science Quarterly*, 53:143, June, 1972.

[7]Jennings, J. T., *Undergraduate Enrollment In Two-Year and Four-Year Colleges*, October, 1972, p. 12.
[8]Withey, S. B., *A Degree and What Else?*, p. 1; Watley, D. J., *Black and Nonblack Youth: Finances and College Attendance*, ERIC, no. ED 052 713, 1971, p. 1.
[9]Pervin, L. A., et. al., "The Dropout...," *op. cit.*, p. 8.
[10]Laird, A. W., "Dropout: Analysis of High Aptitude College Students—Western Kentucky's Search for Clues to this Problem," *Western Kentucky University Faculty Research Bulletin*, p. 95; Pervin, L. A., et. al., "The Dropout...," *op. cit.*, p. 7; Iffert, R. E., *Retention and Withdrawal of College Students*, pp. 4, 17-18.
[11]Astin, A. W., *College Dropouts: A National Profile*, ERIC, no. ED 059 691, February, 1972, p. 49; Jennings, *op. cit.*, p. 12; Richling, John, "70 Per Cent," *Universities Quarterly*, 25:137, Spring, 1971; Berdie, R. F., *Characteristics of Students Today*, ERIC, no. ED 038 090, February, 1966, p. 8; Gustavus, *op. cit.*, p. 136; Kapur, R. L., "Student Wastage At Edinburgh University," *Universities Quarterly*, 26:353, Summer, 1972; Kooker, E. W. and Bellamy, R. Q., "Some Psychometric Differences Between Graduates and Dropouts," *Psychology*, 6:68, May, 1969; Lindsay, C. A., et. al., "Native and transfer baccalaureate students," *Journal of College Student Personnel*, 7:5-13, 1966; Marks, Edmond, "Student Perceptions of College Persistence and Their Intellective, Personality and Performance Correlates," *Journal of Educational Psychology*, 58:211, August, 1967; Rivlin, H. N., et. al., *The First Years In College: Preparing Students For A Successful College Career*, p. 1; Panos, R. J. and Astin, A. W., 5:70, January, 1968; Huber, W. H., "Channeling Students for Greater Retention," *College and University*, 47:19-20, Fall, 1971; Nicholi, A. M., *An Investigation of Harvard Dropouts*, Final Report, ERIC, no. ED 042 068, June
[12]Hornbostel, V. O., et. al., *The Rehabilitation of School Dropouts in Oklahoma City*, p. 22.
[13]Vaizey, *op. cit.*, p. 139; Kapur, *op. cit.*, p. 354; Joff and Adams, "Open Admissions and Academic Quality," *Change*, 3:11, March-April, 1971; Laird, *op. cit.*, pp. 94; George, R. L., and Marshall, J. C., "Personality of Young Adults: College vs. Non-College," *The Journal of College Student Personnel*, 12:438, June, 1971; Rose, H. A., and Elton, C. F., "Another Look At The College Dropout," *Journal of Counseling Psychology*, 13:242, February, 1966; Smith, J. S., "A Multivariate Combination of Academic and Non-Academic Factors Related to Student Attrition," *Dissertation Abstracts International A*, 32:6786-A, June, 1972.

[14]Iffert, R. E. and Clark, B. S., *College Applicants, Entrants, Dropouts*, ERIC, no. ED 055 560, p. 1, 1965, p. 1; Marks, *op. cit.*, p. 211; Vaizey, *op. cit.*, p. 139; Robinson, L. F., *Relation of Student Persistence In College To Satisfaction With Environmental Factors*, p. 154; Thayer, R. E., *Do Low Grades Cause College Students To Give Up*, ERIC, no. ED 054 725, April, 1971, p. 1; Rivlin, *op. cit.*, p. 1; Demos, G. D., "Analysis of College Dropouts—Some Manifest And Covert Reasons," *Personnel and Guidance Journal*, 46:684, 1968; Wagner, E. L., and Sewell, W. H., "Selection and Context as Factors Affecting The Probability of Graduation From College," *American Journal of Sociology*, 75:678, January, 1970.

[15]Yuker, H. E., *et. al.*, *Who Leaves Hofstra For What Reasons*, ERIC, no. ED 065 045, May, 1972, p. 1; Vaizey, *op. cit.*, p. 139.

[16]Dollar, R. J., "Interpersonal Values and College Persistence," *Journal of College Student Personnel*, 11:200, May, 1970; Heath, D. H., *Growing Up In College*, pp. 49-50; Hummel, R. B., *The Development of Intellectual Commitment In University Students*, ERIC, no. ED 063 856, April, 1972, p. 1; Robin and Johnson, "Identifying Potential Dropouts With Class Lists," *Improving College and University Teaching*, 17:178, Summer, 1969; Robinson, *op. cit.*, p. 154; Schein, L. A., "Institutional Characteristics And Student Attitudes," College Student Survey, Winter, 1969, p. 69; Sturtz, S. A., "Age Difference in College Student Satisfaction," *Journal of College Student Personnel*, 12:221, May, 1971.

[17]Marks, *op. cit.*, p. 211; Yuker, *op. cit.*, p. 1; Panos and Astin, *op. cit.*, p. 70.

[18]Nicholi, A. M., *An Investigation of Harvard Dropouts*, ERIC, no. ED 042 068, June, 1970, p. 15.

[19]Chickering, A. W., *Institutional Differences And Student Characteristics*, ERIC, no. ED 014 099, May, 1966, p. 1; Berdie, *op. cit.*, p. 8; Cope, R. G., and Hewitt, R. G., *A Typology of College Student Dropouts: An Environmental Approach*, ERIC, no. ED 030 392, June, 1967, p. 1.

[20]Feldman, K. A., and Newcomb, T. N., *The Impact of College on Students*, pp. 144-145.

[21]Shirey, W. W., *Fieldhouse Enrollments*, 1973, p. 1.

[22]Brown, R. D., *op. cit.*, p. 7.

[23]Chickering, A. W., *Education and Identity*, p. ix.

[24]Gibson, R. C., *The Challenge of Leadership in Higher Education*, pp. 1-362.

[25]Penney, J. F., "Student Personnel Work: A Profession Stillborn," *Personnel and Guidance Journal*, 47:958, 1969.

[26]Trent, J. W. and Medsker, L. L., *Beyond High School: A Study of 10,000 High School Graduates*, p. 126.
[27]Dellenback, John, "Report On Proprietary Vocational Schools," *Congressional Record*, 116:2, August, 1970.
[28]Pervin, "The Later Academic...," *op. cit.*, p. 62.
[29]Cangemi, Joseph Peter, "*Perception Of Students, Faculty And Administrators Regarding Self-Actualization As The Purpose Of Higher Education*, Unpublished doctor's thesis, School of Education, Indiana University, Bloomington, May, 1974, pp. 91-91.
[30]Shannon, J. R., "Percentages of Returns of Questionnaires In Reputable Educational Research," *Journal of Educational Research*, 42:140, October, 1948.
[31]Morely, G. J., *The Science of Educational Research*, p. 253-254; Borg, W. R., and Gall, M. D., *Educational Research An Introduction*, P. 136-137; Kerlinger, F. N., *Foundations of Behavioral Research*, p. 446-447.

Chapter II

REVIEW OF SELECTED RESEARCH AND LITERATURE

The problem of the college dropout has long been of interest to researchers. Numerous studies have been conducted to ascertain the reasons why students withdraw from college before graduation. Many of the reasons for departure from college prior to earning a degree have been categorized into three factors: home influences and background, college environmental influences, and the student's personal, emotional, and academic characteristics.

An individual student brings certain skills with him to his various environments. The student's educational background is a prerequisite for his educational future. In order for the student to be successful in the college environment, he must have skills to fulfill the requirements of that environment. If he has the appropriate skills, the environment becomes a source of reward to him. If he lacks the skills, the environment becomes a source of great dissatisfaction and the probability of withdrawal from that environment is enhanced.[1]

Selection of College

Numerous variables have been found to be related to an individual's college choice and attendance. Primary among these variables are ability, goals, self-concept, sex, place of residence and parents' socioeconomic and educational levels.[2] Elton, Holland, Pervin, Meyerson, and Machlup all have reported research concerning college choice and attendance. In essence, they found personality characteristics influencing the desire to attend a particular college, as well as geographic location, strength of dependence or independence towards parents, commuting distance to college, self-image and the image of the college selected, parental pressures, personal and cultural factors, and lack of knowledge about available educational alternatives.[3]

Characteristics of College Environments

The college environment has been studied by Chickering, Centra, Heath, Hedley, Henry, Kamens, Pervin and Schein. A synthesis of their research indicated that each college had a climate of its own and that this climate attracted a particular type of student. The type of institution selected by a student was a significant factor in determining his college graduation, so was his socioeconomic and intelligence level. Apparently colleges did not meet the interpersonal relationship needs of students. At least students felt their interpersonal needs were not as important on the college campus as were the academic requirements of the institution. Colleges appeared to have different characteristics and these characteristics produced stress for students and decreased their chances for college graduation. When the college characteristics met the students' needs, the probability of graduation increased. The environment found in a College of Arts and Sciences tended to be more oriented toward creativity and intellectual endeavors than did the environment created by the School of Education and the

School of Business in a large Midwestern university. Colleges appeared to discriminate among students on the basis of four variables: sex composition, activities emphasized in which students could become involved, student "elitism"—that is, money and academic ability, and the amount of activism and flexibility (or lack of them) regarding curriculum and social regulations. They were curriculum organization, religious emphasis, patterns of regulation and institutional objectives. Each college seemed to be different from other colleges studied, although colleges in general tend to have certain similarities. The differences in student characteristics found at the different colleges supported the contention that different colleges have dissimilar environments. It was also found that obvious significant differences were found in the characteristics of students attending different kinds of colleges.[4]

Taylor and Hanson[5] stated that achievement was significantly better for a group of engineering freshman living in a homogeneous residence hall when compared with two groups of engineering freshman that were living in various types of environments. The study suggested that the influence of peers with similar interests and similar courses had a strong and positive effect on achievement. DeCoster[6] found that random assignment of students in a dormitory could place the individual in an uncomfortable living atmosphere and create a hinderance to satisfactory academic performance.

Miser,[7] in his study of first year college students and their perceptions of the college environment, found that those whose perception was substantially different from the realities of the college environment which they did in fact experience, earned lower grades than those who had more accurate perceptions of their environment.

Huber[8] stated that the most common criteria for admission into undergraduate programs were quantitative. He suggested that a simplified quantitative approach to admission screening had merit for the purpose of selection and placement of those with the very lowest scores. He agreed that there were many studies that supported the idea that quantitative knowledge played an important part in meeting the criteria for acceptance into undergraduate college. He cautioned, however, that conclusions regarding quantitative indices for undergraduate acceptance were useful only in a rough sense, at the 25 percentile or below. Huber pointed out that over the past three decades, although enrollments have soared, both in terms of the number of students and in terms of the percent of the population, the attrition rate has remained approximately the same.

Hedlund and Jones[9] found that colleges with less students per counselor tended to report higher completion rates than did colleges with a higher student per counselor ratio.

Characteristics of Persisting Students

A serious attempt to delineate outstanding characteristics of the American college graduate was made by the National Opinion Research Center. A survey of 35,000 graduating students yielded the following data.[10]

> The model graduates of June, 1961, were more likely to be men than women, were in their early twenties, came from families where they were neither the youngest nor the oldest, nor the only child, were unmarried, and were white, native-born Americans from cities of over 100,000. They were members of the middle and upper middle class whose fathers and mothers had at least graduated from high school and whose income was over $7,500. Their fathers were managers or professionals. The graduates had at least a part-time job during their final year of college and were still members of the Protestant religion in which they had been raised.
> They had warm and positive feelings toward their schools and professors, planned to continue their education in graduate school (at least eventually), planned to be some kind

of professional (if one counts education from elementary to university as a profession) did not particularly like businessmen, had at least a "B" average, thought of themselves as being in the top one-fourth of their class, and found intellectual and service values the most important things they would look for in their job. While they were in school, they lived in a dormitory or in off-campus housing and were within four hours driving time from their family.

They thought of themselves as conventional, religious, and politically liberal and were inclined to describe themselves as cooperative, ambitious, happy, fun-loving, easy-going, idealistic, athletic and cautious.

Ryle[11] stated that the individual brings to the university environment a set of personal and academic characteristics and goals, as well as specific capacities and weaknesses. The university in turn provides conditions and tasks which are more or less compatible with these student characteristics, goals, capacities and weaknesses. When incompatibility exists, or where certain types of other factors intervene, such as family stress, illness or financial difficulties, the student may fail in terms of meeting the demands of his institution and then will exhibit various symptoms or behaviors, suggesting significant difficulty. At this point, Ryle suggested the university may offer various resources with the aim of helping the student to become reestablished or it may be content to label him a failure and assist him to withdraw from the institution.

Brown[12] found personality and motivation related to perceptions of the collegiate environment. He reported that the parents' portrayal of the campus environment ranked better than did student portrayal. Consensus between parents and students focused on factors of the environment related to campus rules and regulations. Brown reported that students perceived the campus as less academic and more restrictive than did their parents.

Chickering and McCormick[13] found that in personality development and the college experience there were changes that had occurred in most areas measured by the Omnibus Personality Inventory. The amount of change and the direction of the change were quite similar for both men and women as well as for different groups of entering freshmen. It was reported that the direction and amount of change were also similar at all the colleges despite the dramatic differences amongst them. When looking at the different types of students at the different types of colleges, changes were found in attitudes, beliefs and behavior. Chickering and McCormick stated that the diverse institutions of higher education provided safe havens or an appropriate sense of well-being for diverse students. It was reported that those attending college became more autonomous, more complex, more flexible and less materialistic, more aware of their own emotions, more able to express themselves in thought and action, more tolerant of ambiguity, less dogmatic and more intellectually curious. They stated that a student's intellectual competence and breadth may be so limited that he finds it difficult to cope with a college or university academic program. It may contribute very little to his motivation or challenge. At one particular institution of higher education, the nonpersisting students scored significantly higher than the persisting students. Compared to other college students across the country, nonpersisting students were relatively cautious, conservative, conforming and dependent. However, when comparing nonpersisting students with their peers, they were stronger in their impulsiveness, complexity and their need for autonomy. For some students, early withdrawal appears to be necessary. Chickering and McCormick believed that a student's decision to withdraw may be a move in a healthy direction because the withdrawee may be moving toward a more meaningful and challenging environment for himself. It was further stated that colleges can make an important contribution by helping to make the student's withdrawal process a positive experience.

Benezet[14] stated that any college can be a reasonably good institution if the students and the faculty together resolve to make it a worthwhile experience. Based on this, Benezet indicated that it is important for entering students to realize that the primordial requirement to making the educational experience a success is the attitude that a student brings with him to his first year of studies in higher education.

According to Clark[15] students bring with them intellectual equipment, emotional dispositions, interests, motivations, values, attitudes and goals. These characteristics were labeled by Clark and his colleagues as "input variables." These variables are generally ways of viewing experiences, valuing modes of perception, methods of seeking meaning and methods of projecting to the future. Clark stated that input variables are not static, rather they are modified by the environment. Clark added that student characteristics at entrance to college provided a baseline for assessing the ways in which the student will change.

Skager,[16] in evaluating freshmen and sophomore students of ten colleges and universities, found that differences were observed in self-ratings of popularity and scholarship as well as in relation to goals involving religious values, participation in public affairs and making a contribution to science. These differences were observed in relation to the differences in the college studied.

Heywood,[17] determined that the differences between success and failure concerning college revolved around uncertain goals: entering a college other than one's own choice, lack of interest in studies and difficulty in studying. Appel and Witzke's[18] research found freshmen entering college at varying degrees of maturity and some were, therefore, more certain of their future career plans than were others.

Johnston,[19] in attempting to determine characteristics of students living in a quiet residence hall, found marked differences between residents of quiet conventional halls. Residents in the quiet halls were usually older students, upperclassmen who perceived their environment as one characterized by intellectuality, scholastic discipline and consideration for others.

Wagner and Sewell[20] determined that the probability of graduating from college substantially increased with the presence of the following characteristics in students: high intelligence, high ranking in high school classes, high occupational aspirations and high socioeconomic background.

Suczek and Alfert,[21] in investigating the personality development of students in an experimental college program, found a developmental change in the students as defined by personality measures. They found a general liberalization of attitudes on the part of students, making possible a more realistic outlook toward life, greater flexibility in thinking and acting, openness to new experiences and greater compassion in dealing with oneself and others. The educational atmosphere alone was not the most significant factor. Rather, the interaction of the student with certain aspects of the educational atmosphere appeared to be more relevant to student development. They concluded that changes in attitudes will become accelerated in future generations of college students because of rapid cultural changes taking place at this current time.

Sturtz[22] stated that older students generally are more satisfied with college than are younger students. Adult women were found to be generally more satisfied with college and the quality of education. There was generally dissatisfaction among college students regarding college policies and procedures.

Bucklin and Bucklin[23] examined the personality of the persisting student as compared with the nonpersisting student and found that the persisting student tended to have the ability to attack a problem and stick with it, had a strong drive for success and achievement, had a sense of responsibility, was rather contented with the college routine, was conscientious, systematic and diligent in his work habits, was autonomous in thinking and perception, was objective and had a certain strong resemblance to his environment. The persisting student's motivation and interests were highly related to his success. Persisting students tended to have definite vocational plans, came from families interested in higher education and came from families that encouraged the pursuit of higher educational goals and activities. Research by Ikenberry[24] found several of the same characteristics of persisting students as did Bucklin and Bucklin.

Spady[25] stated that students who aspired to finish college were more likely to see themselves through to graduation than those with more modest goals or those who did not have these aspirations. He pointed out that high goals helped one to graduate only when they were clear and realistic.

Research on 54,000 Negro students in New York City indicated that approximately two-thirds of them aspired to obtain a Bachelors or Masters degree and almost 90 percent of them were willing to work full-time in order to stay in college. Over 80 percent of the students involved in the study noted that the reasons for attending an institution of higher learning were to learn more, to get a better job and to fulfill a need for college trained Black people.[26]

Heath[27] reported that part of the college environment involved its interpersonal environment. The personality of one's peers had a significant effect, both directly and indirectly, upon the maturing of an individual on a college campus. The changing atmosphere and expectations within a college also showed effects on students. Students themselves indicated that the type of person with whom they interacted was one of the most important determinants of their personality development. According to Heath, maturation involved the ability of an individual to shape an acceptable degree of adaptation to the demands of both the environment and his own structure needs.

Rose and Elton[28] investigated factors related to persisting and nonpersisting freshmen at the University of Kentucky. Those who withdrew, but remained in good academic standing, were more maladjusted, more hostile, and less interested in academic affairs than were persisters. Persisting students tended to be more submissive to authority and convention than were nonpersisting students. Another study found that persisting students were more programmatically oriented than were nonpersisting students while the latter demonstrated a greater need for independence.[29]

Rossman and Kirk[30] found voluntary withdrawals were better oriented intellectually and had higher ability scores than persisting students at the University of California. Marks[31] reported that persisting students were overly concerned with satisfying parental expectations. They seemed to suffer anxiety and guilt feelings at the prospect of displeasing their parents and found difficulty in resolving conflicts between self and environment. Lehmann[32] suggested that persisting in college was primarily dependent on an individual's intellectual ability. He added, however, that affective factors such as attitude, interest and motivation should not be overlooked.

Turner[33] found a succinct difference between persisting and nonpersisting students:

> Persisters were more selective in choosing their colleges and saw more reasons for attending. They studied harder and were less prone to allow social life to interfere with their studies. They tended to be more intellectual, self-reliant and open-minded before entering college.

He reported that no great significance could be attached to differences in ability or socioeconomic status between the persisting and nonpersisting students. Turner's findings strongly suggested that persisting students entered college with the necessary predispositions.

Astin[34] stated that nearly one-half of all students entering four-year colleges and universities could be classified as persisting students. The dropout rates, according to Astin, at two-year schools were somewhat higher than those of the four-year colleges. The major predictors of success and endurance in college were a student's grades in high school and scores on tests of academic achievement. Other important indicators included being male and a non-smoker, having a high degree of aspiration at the time of college entrance, financial ability particularly on the part of helping parents, scholarships, personal savings and not being employed during the school year.

Kooker and Bellamy[35] stated that baccalaureate recipients were superior to non-holders of the degree in general intelligence, quantitative ability, verbal ability and clerical perceptions. They were found to be more restrained, understanding of others and more thoughtful. They possessed a higher level of reading comprehension, had improved study habits and were more positive in their attitudes toward academic goals.

According to Sandell and Rossman,[36] persisting students generally described their parents favorably and with enthusiasm. Approximately half the persisting students they studied indicated they usually discussed vital concerns with their parents, although they felt they differed from their parents in values, beliefs, goals and life styles. These students claimed to be more liberal, less materialistic and desired an easier way of living.

Chase and Warren[37] found that by the end of the first semester the typical freshman lost some of his confidence regarding his academic ability, although he still considered himself capable of handling academic demands in college. He appeared to want to obtain a marketable skill, while seeking good teachers who would become personally involved with him and who would help him to achieve his skill. He wanted some voice in the university's policy making procedures, wanted advice and counsel when needed and desired autonomy in his personal affairs.

Coker found a significant difference between male and female persisting and nonpersisting college students in the area of vocational role preferences, vocational choice, planned educational major, educational aspirations, number of changes in academic major, place of college residence and size of high school graduating class. Coker's data indicated that being undecided about an educational major may be a positive factor in persisting among male students but may not be a positive factor among female students. Persisting female students planned their vocation in close association with their educational program. In general, Coker observed that persisting students anticipated the completion of their college years as well as future graduate study. The nonpersisting student began college with apparently lower scholastic potential than his persisting counterpart, as well as a lower level of aspiration regarding his future educational and vocational plans. Coker found persistence at college was favored among those who were living in a campus residence hall.[38]

Gelso[39] disputed the often quoted college standard that college students need to spend two hours studying per day for each hour of classroom instruction. His research indicated that in general students studied in the vicinity of one hour per day per subject. Gelso concluded that fewer than 10 percent of the students in college studied two or more hours per day per subject. Students averaged approximately three hours studying per day, but less than three hours per day on typical week days and weekends and more than three hours per day before exams. Resident students studied more than students who commuted.

A study by Hagen[40] provides considerable support to Gelso's findings. Hagen, after synthesizing data on 2,582 college sophomores at 251 colleges and universities, concluded that college students in general spent approximately three hours per day out of class studying their subject matter.

Married students had a more serious attitude toward the challenge of college than single students. Sophisticated female students found college more conforming, group centered and cooperative than male students in general. Members of Greek organizations viewed the college environment as more group oriented than did transfer students.[41]

A recent investigation evaluated the orientation of an institution of higher education regarding self-actualization of students, faculty and administrators as the primary purpose of higher education. The result of the research suggested that students, faculty and administrators were indeed in agreement that moving toward self-actualization was the purpose of higher education. Although students, faculty and administrators were indeed in agreement regarding self-actualization as the purpose of higher education, students were the least interested in self-actualization as the purpose of higher education, while administrators were the most interested in self-actualization as the purpose of higher education. Faculty members appeared to be more interested than students in self-actualization as the purpose of higher education, but not as interested as administrators. Administrators tended to be most concerned with the development of interpersonal relations on a university campus, while students were the least interested in this aspect of higher education.[42]

According to Kuehn,[43] drug use among college students was determined by a multiple and complex set of factors. Students indicated using more than one unlawful drug and cited the drugs used most often were marijuana, amphetamines, LSD and barbiturates. Students expressed the following reasons for the use of drugs: an identification with adults' use of alcohol, tobacco and tranquilizers; feelings of helplessness; discrepancies between ideals of justice, forgiveness and equality; deficiencies in legal and social practices. Kuehn found that student drug users tended to live excessively in present, had an excessive passive and reactive position in interpersonal relationships, demonstrated serious cognitive difficulties, suffered from inexplicable depression, had study difficulties not attributable to reality problems or difficulties in the environment, experienced unrewarding sexual behavior, and overused defensive behavior and rationalization.

A recent study conducted at a major Midwestern university on the use of alcohol and marijuana revealed that 4,425 students (41%) who responded to the survey, 81.4 percent freshmen, 88 percent sophomores, 90.8 percent juniors and 91 percent seniors indicated that they were current users of alcoholic beverages. More specifically, 1.5 percent stated that they drank daily, 45.2 percent drank frequently, 49.8 percent seldom, 1.9 percent only once and 5.7 percent never. Concerning the use of marijuana, the same group of students indicated that 39.3 percent of the freshmen, 45.4 percent of sophomores, 50.1 percent juniors, and 45.8 percent seniors were current users of the drug. Specifically, 22.7 percent of the students surveyed indicated using marijuana frequently, 7.1 percent admitted using it daily, 19.9 percent reported using it seldomly, 5.7 percent stated using it only once, and 43.3 percent reported never using marijuana. The study revealed that 50.3 percent of the students surveyed attributed drug use to social and recreational reasons.[44]

Characteristics of Nonpersisting Students

According to Katz and Sanford,[45] the typical freshman student entered college filled with enthusiasm. However, by the end of the first year, some dropped out and a large number of those that remained were ready for the sophomore slump. Schoonmaker[46] stated that many freshman students were appalled by the impersonal atmosphere they found in college. It seemed they had believed the propaganda about "joining a community of scholars," but suddenly found themselves ignored by their teachers.

Knoell, in a critical review of research on college dropouts, found attrition was but one aspect of the more general phenomenon of persisting or not going to college. Other variables of importance were the institution which the student attended and the system of higher education of which that institution was a part. According to Knoell, withdrawing from college may be viewed as one of the results of the interaction between the student, the institution and interpersonal variables. The major factors associated with attrition were biological, social, academic, motivational, health and financial. Academic ability and achievement were unrelated to attrition, since as many good students as poor ones withdrew from college and since academic difficulties accounted for only 33 percent of dropouts. Knoell[47] explained attrition in the following:

Academic factors, high-school preparation and performances in college; motivation, including both lack of it and changes or conflict in it, and finances emerge most clearly from the literature as important determiners of attrition; illness and injury account for a small but reliable portion of attrition. However, evidence concerning the roles of social factors (such as socio-economic variables and home-town location and size) and personal-social adjustment is still inconclusive.

In recent years there has been additional stress and tension due to greater pressures and competition for admission into college, fierce competition for grades, graduate school placement, and increasing competition for good jobs upon graduation.

Jones and Dennison[48] discovered in their research that all types of students have been found to withdraw from the comprehensive community college and include even those of serious intellectual interests and high academic ability. Recommendations of Jones and Dennison were that college instructors should be better trained in their subject area in order to decrease student dissatisfaction with their college environment. They stated that financial problems were the largest single factor related to the comprehensive community college attrition rate.

Kapur[49] stated that the dropout and the phenomenon of failure in college was multidimensional. There were many facets associated with the decision to withdraw. It was not a simple one-sided dimension. Rather, according to Kapur, dropping out of college involved a number of intellectual, educational, motivational, social and psychological characteristics interacting with characteristics of universities and colleges. There was no single cause of student withdrawal.

Nonpersisting Students: Influence Of Home Environmental Factors

A number of studies suggested that parental influence on children either directly or indirectly was probably as great a factor on nonpersisting students as any other single source.[50] Ridlon reported parents frequently imposed psychological pressures on their children by their own images and attitudes toward college.[51]

Turner[52] stated that parents' social status exerted an important influence on the educational plans of their children. Parents' occupational status also exerted an influence upon college going behavior. Research by Bailey[53] found that of those students who entered college 62.7 percent had parents who were white collar workers. His research also indicated that those students who entered college, 27 percent had parents with agricultural occupations. Goetsch[54] found that when comparing students from different socioeconomic levels, only 20 percent of the lower income families had children who attended college while 90 percent of the superior students from high income backgrounds attended institutions of higher education. He concluded that income and/or low socioeconomic status were highly related in determining whether one attended college.

Parents of dropouts had histories of serious disappointment in their careers, scholastic interruption, mental disorders and other discordant experiences such as divorce, desertion, and death.[55] Parents of persisters in general had fewer of these types of background experiences. Rose and Elton[56] concluded from their study that college dropouts reflected a population of adolescents with diffused (uncertain) identity.

Nonpersisting Students:
Influence of College Environmental Factors

The college environment imposes varied social and intellectual challenges upon its students. As an individual moves along Havighurst's ladder of developmental tasks, he is faced with unique challenges and conflicts. Several studies have found that almost all students are exposed to stress upon entering college.[57]

Cope and Hewitt[58] researched the environmental press (stress) approach and its effect on students and found there were major pressures within the environment of colleges and universities that confronted students. The two major presses were social and academic; a third may be religious. Since students experienced difficulties in meeting with these presses, whether separately or with a number of them simultaneously, they may be encouraged to withdraw.

Thistlethwaite[59] stated that the college environment was a vital factor in determining the student's motivation to pursue higher intellectual development. Also, factors in the natural sciences seemed to differ from those which motivated success in the arts, humanities and social sciences.

Rivlin[60] found that the freshman year in college was disastrous for most students. Even the bright and eager students often found the first year difficult and many of them were forced to withdraw. Upon arriving at college, students were faced with a strange new world. Rivlin noted that one of the common problems for most students was that they lacked familiarity with what to expect in a college environment and they lacked the necessary background of preparation and knowledge to make successful adaptation to the new environment.

Pace[61] considered the concept that cultures in higher education may be viewed as a system of complex environmental presses, practices and policies which may be related to a similar complex of personal needs.

Robin and Johnson[62] stated that in any list of reasons regarding the college dropout was failure of the marginal students to adjust to the impersonal atmosphere of a college or university because of the lack of communication between students and their professors. It was apparent that many promising students left the academic environment forever when they might have survived and even improved if they only had the proper attention and guidance from an understanding and helpful professor. The floundering student usually failed to discuss his problems with his professors and manifested difficulties by not attending classes; as a consequence, he increased his problems and the potential for withdrawal.

According to Landrith,[63] at least half of the students entering junior colleges withdrew prior to completing their two-year studies. The key to the problem was related to the faculty of the specific institution. Both junior college and four-year college faculty failed to understand and empathize with what the student was trying to accomplish in his first and second year of college.

Turner[64] stated withdrawal was due to a number of reasons related to the personal characteristics of the student, as well as a mismatch between the student and the institution's environmental factors. Turner found that potential withdrawees displayed certain identifiable characteristics, such as disinterest and noninvolvement in college affairs, doubtful vocational goals, rigidity in attitudes, intolerance toward conformity, inadequate adjustment, unrealistic image of college life, unsatisfactory attendance, high level anxiety, fear of change and social introversion.

Nonpersisting Students:
Influence of Personal and Academic Characteristics

Savicki,[65] in researching the effects of various factors on withdrawal and achievement of college students, reported that students who withdrew from college for various reasons were psychologically different from those students who continued in college.

Hannah[66] found that thoughts regarding withdrawal from colleges and universities occurred during periods of anxiety and stress related to college exams and papers. He further stated that the actual decision to depart from college was made while students were away from campus when feelings of adequacy and relief were high and other practical and noncollegiate influences were more strongly felt. According to Hannah, dropouts had little introspective ability, had considerable anger toward their parents, seemed to have positive attitudes regarding a plan different from that of college attendance and had strong peer ties while in college.

Reik[67] explained dropping out of college in terms of the conflict of what is expected from the individual by society and what the individual expected in return from life and society. He also stated that generally society and parents alike viewed a student's withdrawing from college as failure or a waste of talent. Levenson,[68] from a somewhat different perspective, described withdrawal from college or a university as a psychosocial manifestation of the individual's identity crisis that may be looked at as a way of resolving the crisis and searching for a more meaningful life. He added that such behavior created stress and threat to the dropout's parents, peers and teachers since his behavior reflected on their lives.

Saranoff[69] reported a number of highly complex and significant phenomena of underachievement. He summarized a rather typical case of a failing student:

> . . . an immature, tensional, and inert person lacking in mature motivation for college work and appreciation of educational values, and without constructively worked out vocational goals. Moreover, he was plagued by intense feelings of inadequacy as a consequence of unresolved sibling rivalry with an older brother. His emotional liabilities were increased by anxiety over his makeup and tended to recoil from the challenge of a university curriculum. Thus, in spite of superior intellectual endowment, his study habits were very insufficient. He fell behind early in the semester, and when confronted with the fact that he was failing, tended to become more negligent in meeting assignments. In this regard, his participation in the marching band was an added impetus toward failure since it was a drain on his time and energy, especially during the first and for him the most crucial half of the semester. Finally, poor interpersonal relations with his roommate made it more difficult for him to study in his room with any real effectiveness.

Hannah[70] found college dropouts were more complex, more impulsive, more anxious, less altruistic, less personally integrated and less willing to exert an effort to make a good impression on either peers or their instructors. They were anxious about their environment and about themselves. They had a high need for independence and apparently sought ways to test that need. These students withdrew from college probably because of their uncertain feelings and because of lack of direction about themselves and their environment.

Rigidity in thought and action were found to be among the contributing factors leading to college withdrawal. In addition, students who had social and academic difficulties before entering college had a greater tendency to withdraw from college.[71] Rose and Elton[72] observed that anxiety, hostility, maladjustment, nonconformity, low interest in literature, dislike for abstract thought, and diverse values were significantly related to leaving college. Nicholi,[73] at Harvard University, determined psychiatric consultation was four times as frequent among Harvard dropout students as it was among the student population in general. According to Nicholi, depression seemed to play a significant role in a student's decision to leave the academic environment. Surprisingly, 39 percent of the students withdrew because of emotional disorders.

Bucklin and Bucklin[74] stated that the nonpersisting student tended not to have the ability to stick with a given task, appeared to be less satisfied with a college routine, was less sure of the role the college would play in his future, seemed to be less able to distinguish the important from the unimportant, and was less effective and diligent in carrying out his daily activities. The college dropout tended to be a careless test-taker, often was lacking in the ability to adapt to the college environment, had a serious deficit of self-discipline, and had a family that did not support his educational endeavors. He tended to be rigid, opinioned, inflexible, non-academically oriented and distrustful of adult authority. He preferred social activity to studying. He had ill-defined goals and was uncertain of his occupational choice and college major. Bucklin and Bucklin reported that students who had definite goals tended to have higher S.A.T. verbal scores, had a higher grade point average in high school and finished in the upper ranks of their high school class. Studies by Bucklin and Bucklin and Ikenberry found that nonpersisting students had lower secondary school grades and had significantly lower test scores in the reading area and academic ability.[75] The values of the nonpersisting student tended to be different from those of the persisting student. The nonpersisting student appeared to have the goal of immediate reward; he sought an immediate payoff for his energies, whereas the persisting student was less interested in immediate gratification and could postpone gratification for some future time.[76]

Zaccaria and Creaser's[77] research supported the hypothesis that personality characteristics of students withdrawing from a university or college were not necessarily indicative of emotional disturbance or maladjustment but could be an expression of developmental needs which could not be fulfilled within the university environment. An unsatisfactory academic record was the major factor which contributed to voluntary as well as involuntary withdrawal.

Chickering and Hannah discovered that the most important determinants of withdrawal were academic underachievement, academic difficulty, discrepancy between the college's proposed beliefs and the actual behavior found there, dislike of the general college atmosphere, a strong feeling of discomfort and a more positive impression regarding another school.[78] Emotional turmoil and stress frequently accompanied students who left school before graduating. Feelings of failure, anxiety about the future, depression, rebelliousness and anger generally existed in those who withdrew from the academic environment. Their life style was clouded, their religious beliefs, values and attitudes were also unsettled, shifting and unclear. They appeared to be in a state of flux. The atmosphere of the college was perceived as dead. The student believed that no one was really interested in him, his ideas, or even in social issues. Some students gradually drifted into withdrawing, while others broke loose more suddenly and set off for what they believed were more clear purposes and goals. Chickering and Hannah concluded that ten of the most frequently mentioned topics by students who were considering withdrawal from college were: (1) academic underachievement or difficulty, (2) educational plans and purposes, (3) vocational plans, (4) religious beliefs, (5) attitudes and values, (6) financial problems, (7) plans concerning life in general, (8) college rules and regulations, (9) limited offering in college programs, and (10) educational opportunities elsewhere.

Landis[79] researched the problems related to college withdrawal by reviewing the problems 238 students mentioned in their autobiographies. He concluded that it was possible to predict fairly closely the specific problems that would be disturbing freshman students on college campuses as well as in the future. Specific problems included: inferiority complex, daydreaming, compensating for inferiority feelings, disillusionment in changing from the small local group to the larger group, sex problems, feelings of insecurity, undesirable traits of temperament, introversion, religious problems, death in family, personal fear, emancipating oneself from home, disillusionment with friends and adults, financial difficulties, family conflicts, shifting from rural to city living, superiority complex, conflict over college rules and regulations, moral disillusionment, hero or idol worship, revolt against authority, sensitiveness, homesickness, parents forcing their wishes or ambitions on me, inability to take responsibility and make decisions, conflict with previous and new attitudes and beliefs, rivalry with brothers and sisters, not being accepted by fraternity or sorority, divorce of parents, and foster home problems.

It has been said often that the high school dropout is uniquely a product of his environment. The following characteristics are symptoms suggesting potential withdrawal from high school. It appears also that college dropouts have many of the same characteristics as do high school dropouts. The information in Table 2

TABLE 2. SIMILAR CHARACTERISTICS OF HIGH SCHOOL AND COLLEGE DROPOUTS

Characteristics	High School Dropouts	College Dropouts
Division and discord in family life	X	X
Parents formerly dropouts	X	X
Lack of parental encouragement	X	X
Inadequate high school preparation		X
Faulty introduction in beginning college orientation		X
Consistent failure to achieve in regular school work	X	X
Low native ability	X	X
Poor study habits	X	X
Disinterest in school work	X	X
Pregnancy	X	
Retention	X	
Frequent absence and tardiness	X	X
Avoiding participation in extracurricular activities	X	X
Poor self-concept	X	X
Peer and social problems	X	X
Sex problems	X	
Lack of self-confidence	X	X
Record of delinquency	X	
Resentful, defiant	X	
Personal difficulties		X
Lack of self-discipline	X	X
Poor student-teacher relationship	X	X
Unwise curricular choice		X
Enrolled for social rather than academic reasons		X
Uncertain educational and vocational goals	X	X
Influenced by immediate rewards rather than distant rewards	X	X

was based upon a review of the literature and presents some of the common characteristics shared by high school and college dropouts.[80]

Based on a review of the literature, it was apparent that the college dropout exhibited many common factors shared by the high school dropout.[81] The factors associated with a student withdrawing from high school became more complex and compounded once a student entered college.

A study comparing a group of nonpersisting students with a group of persisting students in performance on cognitive and personality factors described the nonpersisting students as more likely to be emotionally disturbed, impulsive, lacking educational commitment and unable to learn from past experiences.[82]

Kooker and Bellamy[83] concluded that graduation as opposed to nongraduation was related to students' anticipated grades, ability estimation, campus organizational membership, vocational goals, attitudes toward coming to college and educational level of both parents.

Barkey's[84] study revealed that there was direct correlation between grade point average and use of library. Kramer and Kramer[85] found a statistically significant difference in library usage between persisting and nonpersisting students. Of those freshman students who frequented the library and took out at least one book, only 26 percent withdrew. Of those who failed to use the library, 43 percent did not return the following year.

Vener[86] stated that scholastic ability, socioeconomic status, and previous high school experience played a vital role in influencing one's future in higher education. Vener's study found 61 percent of the students at the top quartile of academic ability expressed plans to attend college, while only 24 percent at the bottom quartile showed similar desires.

Ridlon[87] stated the college dropout rate increased at the very time high schools were sending the best of their classes to college. The answer for students' ineffectiveness was found in reading skills and personal attitudes (self-consciousness, fear, anxiety, selfishness, aggressiveness, timidity and lethargy).

Research by Fox[88] concerned itself with the efficient use of study habits by college students. The results of poor study habits were both a cause and a consequence of what was often viewed as personal maladjustment. A study by Roid[89] reported that college tests and exams greatly influenced the emotions of students. Lack of confidence either prior to or after a test destroyed students' motivation to study.

Yuker[90] found that the average grade point average and the scholastic majors selected by nonpersisting students at Hofstra University were not different from that of the rest of the student body. The major reasons given for withdrawal were personal, financial, dormitory reasons, unhappiness with nonacademic factors and dissatisfaction with academic factors. Poorer students cited personal and financial reasons, whereas the academically better student cited dissatisfaction with the dorms and other nonacademic variables at the university as influential factors for withdrawal.

According to Smith,[91] desire to maintain a high academic record appeared to be the main difference between persisting and nonpersisting students. Family social status and family independence were important motivational factors virtually in every case when differences between persisting and nonpersisting students were viewed. Female dropouts tended to be underachieving due to factors such as independence and non-conformity, which repressed their motivation to obtain better grades. Both male and female persisting students seemed to be capable and motivated. Persisting students developed more social concern, liberalism and non-conformity.

Past research done at this major Midwestern university has been primarily concerned with either persisting or nonpersisting students. These studies generally were concerned with such factors as perceptions of the college environment by entering freshmen during orientation week,[92] comparison of the perceptions of students in general attending three different colleges within the university,[93] the influence of environment upon grade point average,[94] a study of body types, self-image and environmental adjustment in freshman females,[95] characteristics and performance of regional campus transfer students,[96] comparison of females majoring in three different colleges,[97] identification of attitudes among undergraduates,[98] and the influence of general factors upon students that withdrew.[99]

In summary, many factors have been related to success and failure in college. Some are concerned with preparation for the collegiate experience. From research, a variety of factors have been identified which differentiate persisting students from nonpersisting students. Persisting students were more mature, flexible, selective in choosing their school and more certain about their educational goals. They had a greater sense of self-awareness, self-motivation, better study habits, self-management and self-discipline, greater parental support and financial security, less parental pressures, higher aspirations, greater endurance, interest in school and possessed greater intellectual and academic abilities. The nonpersisting students frequently suffered from poor motivation, inadequate work habits, uncertain goals, disinterest in school, and immaturity in attitudes and perceptions. They have low level status and achievment drives, lack self-initiative, have financial difficulties, are poor decision makers, are disorganized and lack intellectual independence. They are procrastinators when faced with academic responsibilities and are often unable to identify with or to become involved in college life and related campus activities.

REFERENCES

[1]Starr, Ann, *et. al.*, "Differences in college students satisfaction: Academic dropouts, nonacademic dropouts, and nondropouts," *Journal of Counseling Psychology*, 19:318, 322, April, 1972; Chase, C. I., "The College Dropout: High School Prologue," *Bulletin of the National Association of Secondary School Principals*, 54:66, January-May, 1970.

[2]Medsker, L. L., and Trent, J. W., "Factors Related to Type of College Attended," pp. 41-50, in *College And Students: Selected Readings In The Social Psychology of Higher Education*, p. 42; Elton, C. F., "Personality of Low Income Males: College Versus Noncollege," *Journal of College Student Personnel*, 11:210, May, 1970; Bailey, B. H., *Characteristics of High School Seniors As Related To Subsequent College Attendance*, pp. 82-83; George and Marshall, "Personality of Young Adults: College vs. Non-College," *The Journal of College Student Personnel*, 12:438, Nov., 1971; Chase, C. I., "The College Dropout. . . ," *op. cit.*, pp. 66-67; Stordahl, K. E., *Influences On College Choice*, ERIC, no. ED 031 143, April, 1968, p. 1.

[3]Elton, *op. cit.*, p. 210; Holland, J. L., "Student Explanations of College Choices and Their Relation to College Popularity, College Productivity and Sex Differences," *College and University*, 33:319-320, Spring, 1958; Pervin, L. A., *Dissatisfaction With College And The College Dropout: A Transactional Report*, ERIC, no. ED 021 335, August, 1967; Meyerson, Martin, "The Ethos of the American College Student: Beyond the Protests," pp. 266-291, in *The Contemporary University*, edited by R. S. Morrison, 1966, p. 269; Machlup, Fritz, "Longer Education, Thinner, Broader, or Higher," *A G B Reports*, 14:11, September, 1971.

[4]Chickering, A. W., *Institutional Differences and Student Characteristics*, ERIC, no. ED 014 099, May, 1966, pp. 1, 12; Centra, J. A., "How Students Perceive Their College Environments," *College Board Review*, 79:13, Spring, 1971; Heath, D. H., *Growing Up In College*, pp. 74-75; Hedley, W. H., "Freshman Survival And Attrition At A Small, Private Liberal Arts College: A Discriminant Analysis of Intellectual and Non-Intellectual Variables," *Dissertation Abstracts*, 10;959, 1968; Henry, J. L., *Student Characteristics And Perception of Indiana University*, Unpublished doctor's thesis, School of Education, Indiana University, Bloomington, June, 1966, p. 168; Kamens, D. H., "The College Charter And College Size: Factors On Occupational Choice and College Attrition," *Sociology of Education*, 44:270-271, Summer, 1971; Pervin, L. A., *Dissatisfaction With College And The College Dropout: A Transactional Report*, ERIC, no. ED 021 335, August, 1967, pp. 1, 28; Schein, *op. cit.*, p. 69.

[5]Taylor, R. G., and Hanson, G. R., "Environmental Impact On Achievement and Study Habits," *The Journal of College Student Personnel*, 12:453, November, 1971.

[6]DeCoster, D. A., "Effects of Homogeneous Housing Assignments For High Ability Students," *The Journal of College Student Personnel*, 9:75, April, 1968.

[7]Miser, K. M., *The Impact of The First Semester of College On Student Perceptions Of The College Environment And Its Relationship To Academic Achievement And Personal Development*, Unpublished doctor's thesis, School of Education, Indiana University, Bloomington, June, 1971, p. 123.

[8]Huber, W. H., "Channeling Students For Greater Retention," *College and University*, 47:19-20, Fall, 1971.

[9]Hedlund, D. E., and Jones, T. J., "Effect of Student Personnel Services On Completion Rate In Two-Year Colleges," *The Journal of College Student Personnel*, 11:198, May, 1970.

[10]Vener, A. M., "College Education and Vocational Career," pp. 100-116, in *The College Student*, by W. B. Brookover, et. al., 1965, pp. 108-109.

[11]Ryle, A., "Student Health and Student Wastage," *Universities Quarterly*, 25:162-163, Spring, 1971.

[12]Brown, R. D., *Parental Perceptions of University Life and Their Characterizations of Their Sons and Daughters*, ERIC, no. ED 038 699, 1970, pp. 3, 5.

[13]Chickering, A. W., and McCormick, John, *Personality Development And The College Experience*, ERIC, no. ED 042 402, 1970, pp. 1, 17.

[14]Benezet, L. T., "College Study: Expectations and Realities," pp. 1-21, in *The First Years In College: Preparing Students For A Successful College Career*, edited by H. N. Rivlin, et. al., 1965, pp. 6-7.

[15]Clark, B. R., et. al., *Students and Colleges: Interaction and Change*, 1972, pp. 142-143.

[16]Skager, R., *Changes In Self-Ratings and Life Goals Among Students With Different Characteristics*, ERIC, no. ED 014 095, August, 1966, p. 1.

[17]Heywood, John, "A Report On Student Wastage," *Universities Quarterly*, 25:189, 202-204, Spring, 1971.

[18]Appel, V. H., and Witzke, D. B., *Goal Orientations. Self-Orientation: Two Perspectives Affecting Indecision About Collegiate Major and Career Choice*, ERIC, no. ED 063 455, April, 1972, p. 1.

[19]Johnston, Sylvia, *A Comparison of Environmental Perceptions of Student Subgroups In Residence Halls*, ERIC, no. ED 053 667, Dec., 1971, p. 1.

[20]Wagner, E. L., and Sewell, W. H., "Selection and Context As Factors Affecting The Probability of Graduation From College," *American Journal of Sociology*, 95:678, January, 1970.

[21]Suczek, Robert, and Alfert, Elizabeth, *Personality Development In Two Different Educational Atmospheres*, ERIC, no. ED 042 074, August, 1970, pp. 130-132.

[22]Sturtz, S. A., "Age Differences In College Student Satisfaction," *The Journal of College Student Personnel*, 12:221-222, May, 1971.

[23]Bucklin, R. W., and Bucklin, M. L., *The Psychological Characteristics of the College Persistor and Leaver: A Review*, ERIC, no. ED 049 709, August, 1970, pp. 1, 12.

[24]Ikenberry, S. O., "Factors in College Persistence," *Journal of Counseling Psychology*, 8:322, Winter, 1969.

[25]Spady, W. G., "Dropouts from Higher Education: An Interdisciplinary Review and Synthesis," *Interchange*, 1:72, April, 1970.

[26]National Scholarship Service and Fund For Negro Students, *A National Profile of Black Youth, Class of 1971*, ERIC, no. ED 066 120, Jan., 1972, p. 1.

[27]Heath, *op. cit.*, pp. 49-50.

[28]Rose, H. A., and Elton, C. F., "Another Look At the College Dropout," *Journal of Counseling Psychology*, 13:244, Summer, 1966.

[29]Suczek, Robert and Alfert, Elizabeth, *Personality Characteristics of College Dropouts*, p. 1.

[30]Rossman, J. E., and Kirk, B. A., "Factors Related to Persistence and Withdrawal Among University Students," *Journal of Counseling Psychology*, 17:56, January, 1970.

[31]Marks, Edmond, "Student Perceptions of College Persistence and Their Intellective, Personality and Performance Correlates," *Journal of Educational Psychology*, 58:220, August, 1967.

[32]Lehmann, I. J., "American College Students and the Socialization Process," pp. 58-77, in *The College Student*, edited by W. B. Brookover, *et. al.*, p. 63.

[33]Turner, H. J., Jr., *The Half That Leaves: A Limited Survey of Attrition In Community Colleges*, ERIC, no. ED 038 607, March, 1970, p. 4.

[34]Astin, A. W., *College Dropouts: A National Profile*, ERIC, no. ED 059 691, February, 1972, pp. 1 and 49.

[35]Kooker, E. W., and Bellamy, R. Q., "Some Psychometric Differences Between Graduates and Dropouts," *Psychology: A Journal of Human Behavior*, 6:68, May, 1969.

[36]Sandell, S. A., and Rossman, J. E., "College Freshman View Their Parents," *Personnel and Guidance Journal*, 49:822-824, June, 1971.

[37]Chase, C. I., and Warren, S., *Freshmen View The College Scene: Opinions Before And After The Initial Semester*, ERIC, no. ED 029 592, 1969, p. 1.

[38]Coker, D. L., *Diversity Of Intellective And Non-Intellective Characteristics Between Persisting And Non-Persisting Students Among Campuses*, ERIC, no. ED 033 645, April, 1968, pp. 1, 106-110.

[39]Gelso, C. J., "Some Findings About Student Study Patterns," *College Student Survey*, 3:52,54, Winter, 1969.

[40]Hagen, E. W., *The Sophomore Norming Sample for the General Examinations of the Comprehensive College Tests*, Educational Testing Service, Princeton, N. J., 1964.

[41]Duling, J. A., "Differences In Perceptions of the Environmental Press By Selected Student Sub-Groups," *Journal of the National Association of Women Deans and Counselors*, 32:130-132, 1968.

[42]Cangemi, J. P., *Perceptions Of Students, Faculty And Administrators*

Regarding Self-Actualization As The Purpose of Higher Education, Unpublished doctor's thesis, School of Education, Indiana University, Bloomington, May, 1974, p. 73.
[43]Kuehn, J. L., "The Student Drug User and His Family," *The Journal of College Student Personnel*, 11:409-11, November, 1970.
[44]Crowe, J., *Indiana University Drug Study*, p. 28.
[45]Katz, Joseph and Sanford, Nevitt, "Curriculum and Personality," pp. 121-132, in *College and Character*, edited by Nevitt Sanford, 1964, p. 126.
[46]Schoonmaker, A. N., "The Freshman Year," pp. 103-113, in *A Students Survival Manual*, 1971, p. 104.
[47]Knoell, D. M., "A Critical Review of Research On The College Dropout," *The College Dropout And The Utilization Of Talent*, pp. 63-81, edited by Lawrence A. Pervin, *et. al.*, 1966, pp. 63 and 65.
[48]Jones, Gordon and Dennison, J. D., *A Comparative Study of Persister and Non-Persister College Students*, ERIC, no. ED 062 975, June, 1972, pp. 1, 66 and 67.
[49]Kapur, R. L., "Student Wastage At Edinburgh University: Factors Related To Failure And Dropout," *Universities Quarterly*, 26:354, Summer, 1972.
[50]Greenshields, M. J., "The College Going Decision: High School Seniors Give Their Reasons," College and University, 32:210, Winter, 1957; Trent, J. W., and Medsker, L. L., *Beyond High School: A Study of 10,000 High School Graduates*, pp. 41-42.
[51]Ridlon, H. G., "Why Freshmen Fail," pp. 12-20, in *Introduction To College Life*, by N. T. Bell, 1966, p. 19.
[52]Turner, *op. cit.*, p. 2.
[53]Bailey, *op. cit.*, pp. 85.
[54]Goetsch, H. B., *Parental Income And College Opportunities*, pp. 88-89.
[55]Levenson, E. A., *et. al.*, "Family Transaction In The Etiology of Dropping Out of College," *Contemporary Psychoanalysis*, 3:134, February, 1967.
[56]Rose, and Elton, *op. cit.*, pp. 99-100.
[57]Pervin, L. A., *et. al.*, "The Dropout In Conflict With Society," pp. 3-21, in *The College Dropout And The Utilization of Talent*, edited by L. A. Pervin, *et. al.*, p. 15; Dollar, R. J., "Interpersonal Values and College Persistence," *The Journal of College Student Personnel*, 11:200, May, 1970; Blaine, G. B. *et. al.*, *Emotional Problems of the Students*, pp. 66, 98.
[58]Cope, R. G., and Hewitt, R. G., *A Typology of College Dropouts: An Environmental Approach*, ERIC, no. ED 030 392, June, 1969, p. 14.
[59]Thistlethwaite, D. L., "College Press and Student Achievement," *Journal of Educational Psychology*, 50:190, October, 1959.
[60]Rivlin, H. N., *et. al.*, *The First Years In College: Preparing Students For A Successful College Career*, p. v.

[61]Pace, R. C., and Stern, G. B., "An Approach To The Measurement of Psychological Characteristics of College Environments," *Journal of Educational Psychology*, 49:269, October, 1958.

[62]Robin, Burton, and Johnson, Philip, "Identifying Potential Dropouts With Class Lists," *Improving College and University Teaching*, 17:178, Summer, 1969.

[63]Landrith, H. F., "Two-Year Colleges: Prescription for Junior College Dropouts," *School and Society*, 49:49, January, 1971.

[64]Turner, *op. cit.*, pp. 6-8.

[65]Savicki, V., *et. al.*, "Student Role Orientations And College Dropouts," *Journal of Counseling Psychology*, 17:559-560, June, 1970.

[66]Hannah, W., "Withdrawal from College," *The Journal of College Student Personnel*, 10:398, November, 1969.

[67]Reik, L. E., "The College Dropout in Clinical Perspective," pp. 177-187, in *The College Dropout And The Utilization Of Talent*, edited by L. A. Pervin, *et. al.*, 1966, pp. 178, 182.

[68]Levenson, *op. cit.*, p. 134.

[69]Saranoff, Irving and Theophile, Raphael, "Five Failing College Students," pp. 289-328, in *Underachievement*, by M. Kornrich, 1965, p. 296.

[70]Hannah, W., "Personality Differences. . . ," *op. cit.*, p. 19.

[71]Gibson, R. L., *et. al.*, "The High School Dropout Goes to College," *Personnel and Guidance Journal*, 45:827, April, 1967.

[72]Rose, H., and Elton, C. F., "Another Look At. . . ," *op. cit.*, p. 242.

[73]Nicholi, A. M., *An Investigation of Harvard. . .*, *op. cit.*, pp. 3, 15.

[74]Bucklin and Bucklin, *op. cit.*, pp. i, 1, 12, 13.

[75]Bucklin and Bucklin, *ibid*, pp. 12-13; Ikenberry, S. O., "Factors in College Persistence," *Journal of College Psychology*, 8:322, Winter, 1961.

[76]Bucklin and Bucklin, *op. cit.*, pp. 12-13.

[77]Zaccaria, Lucy and Creaser, James, "Factors related to persistence in an urban commuter university," *The Journal of College Student Personnel*, 12:286, 290, July, 1971.

[78]Chickering, A. W., and Hannah, W., "The Process of Withdrawal," *Liberal Education*, 55:551-553, December, 1969.

[79]Landis, P. H., "A Personal Inventory," pp. 9-22, in *So This Is College*, pp. 10-11.

[80]Cangemi, J. P., and Coan, D. L., "A Clinical Method For Identifying Potential Dropouts," *College Student Journal*, 7:78-82, January-February, 1973; Kowalski, C. J., and Cangemi, J. P., "High School Dropouts: A Lost Resource," *College Student Journal*, 8: 71-74, Nov.-Dec., 1974.

[81]Kowalski and Cangemi, *op. cit.*, pp. 73-74.

[82]Vaughan, R. P., "College Dropouts: Dismissed vs. Withdrew," *Personnel and Guidance Journal*, 46:685, 688, March, 1968.
[83]Kooker and Bellamy, *op. cit.*, p. 68.
[84]Barkey, Patrick, "Patterns of Student Use of a College Library," *College and Research Libraries*, 26:115, March, 1965.
[85]Kramer, L. A., and Kramer, M. B., "The College Library and The Dropout," *College and Research Libraries*, 29:310, July, 1968.
[86]Vener, *op. cit.*, p. 105.
[87]Ridlon, *op. cit.*, p. 96.
[88]Fox, L., "Effecting the Use of Efficient Study Habits," *Journal of Methetics*, 1:75076, 1962.
[89]Roid, G. H., *Training, Self-Management and Study Habits in College Students*, 1971-1972, p. 26.
[90]Yuker, H. E., et. al., *Who Leaves Hofstra For What Reasons*, ERIC, no. ED 065 045, May, 1972, p. 1.
[91]Smith, J. S., "A Multivariate Combination of Academic and Non-Academic Factors Related to Student Attrition," *Dissertation Abstracts International*, 32:6786-A, June, 1972.
[92]Miser, *op. cit.*, p. 123.
[93]Henry, *op. cit.*, p. 168.
[94]Steedly, G. F., *Differences In Perception. . .*, *op. cit.*, p. 64.
[95]Alexander, R. H., *A Study of Body Types, Self-Image, And Environmental Adjustment In Freshman College Females*, Unpublished doctor's thesis, School of Education, Indiana University, Bloomington, June, 1967, p. 63-64.
[96]Hughes, A. L., *Diversity of Characteristics. . . ,op. cit.* p. 102.
[97]Greenleaf, E. A., *A Comparison of Women At Indiana University Majoring In Three Different Colleges*, Unpublished doctor's thesis, School of Education, Indiana University, Bloomington, August, 1952, p. 148.
[98]Hancock, B. A., *Undergraduate Students Attitudes and Factors Influencing Attitudes*, Unpublished doctor's thesis, School of Education, Indiana University, Bloomington, June, 1971, p. 99.
[99]Koelsche, C. L., *A Study Of The Student Drop-Out Problem At Indiana University*, Unpublished doctor's thesis, School of Education, Indiana University, Bloomington, August, 1953, p. 164.

Chapter III

ANALYSIS OF DATA

The analysis of the data collected is presented in two sections in this chapter. In the first section an overview of all the data comparing persisting and nonpersisting students is presented. The second section deals only with significant items in which the inferential statistic chi-square was utilized. Interpretations and explanations were provided for each section of the data presented.

The research focused on the differences between the home environment, college environment, and the personal, emotional and academic characteristics of the persisting and nonpersisting students at a major Midwestern university. Individuals in the random population selected for this research were compared on the basis of their responses to each item in the questionnaire.

Comparative Data

Home environment. Information relevant to the home environment is displayed in Table 3. The home environmental factors

TABLE 3. HOME ENVIRONMENTAL FACTORS FOR PERSISTING AND NONPERSISTING STUDENTS

Items	Persisting N = 201 f	%	Nonpersisting N = 165 f	%	Chi-Square & Probability
Number of children in family:					
1 child	10	5	8	4.8	$X^2 =$ .2435
2 or 3 children	106	52.7	83	50.3	$p =$ .8854
4 or more children	85	42.3	74	44.8	
Parents' status:					
separated	14	7.0	15	9.1	$X^2 =$ .9502
married	170	85.0	134	81.2	$p =$ .6218
deceased	16	8.0	16	9.7	
Father's educational level:					
high school or lower	70	34.8	89	53.9	$X^2 =$ 19.2310
up to 2 years of college	18	9.0	14	8.5	$p =$ .0007**
up to Bachelor's degree	64	31.8	46	27.3	
up to Master's degree	30	14.9	12	7.9	
doctorate or equivalent	19	9.5	4	2.4	
Mother's educational level:					
high school or lower	104	51.7	105	63.6	$X^2 =$ 6.0025
up to 2 years of college	21	10.4	14	8.5	$p =$ .1115
up to Bachelor's degree	47	23.4	32	19.4	
up to Master's degree	29	14.4	14	8.5	
doctorate or equivalent	0	0	0	0	
Problems at home:					
financial	43	21.5	44	26.7	$X^2 =$ 1.0601
					$p =$ .3032
health or medical	12	6.0	23	13.9	$X^2 =$ 5.6897
					$p =$ .0171*
personal	45	22.5	55	33.3	$X^2 =$ 4.8037
					$p =$ .0284*
none or other	116	58.0	83	50.3	$X^2 =$ 3.1512
					$p =$ .2069

f = frequency counts, % = percentages, X^2 = chi-squares, p = probability scores.
* <.05
** <.01

were number of children in the family, parents' marital status, father's and mother's educational level, and problems at home.

Analysis of the data in Table 3 indicated three items were found to differentiate significantly the persisting from the nonpersisting students. These factors were father's educational level, health or medical problems and personal problems at home.

Little difference was found between the number of children in the family of the persisting and nonpersisting students. With regard to parental marital status, a slightly greater percentage of the nonpersisting students' parents were either separated or deceased. The data also indicated that a greater percentage of the mothers of the persisting students in comparison with the mothers of the dropouts had at least 2 years of college education. Interestingly none of the mothers of the persisting and nonpersisting students had a doctoral degree. Finally, nonpersisting students expressed a slightly greater percentage of financial home problems than did persisting students.

College environment. Information relevant to the college environment and its influence on persisting and nonpersisting students is located in Tables 4, 5, and 6. Table 4 contains information related to the students' satisfaction with the atmosphere and living conditions.

Data in Table 4 indicated a significant difference between persisting and nonpersisting students and their satisfaction with the general atmosphere at school. Persisting students expressed a greater satisfaction with the general atmosphere.

The students were asked to express their satisfaction with their living conditions. The nonpersisting students indicated a slightly greater dissatisfaction with their college living conditions than did the persisting students.

Information indicating the need to talk with the academic advisors and faculty members and the evaluation of their attitudes is displayed in Table 5. Students responded by checking "unconcerned," "slightly concerned" or "concerned" regarding their perceived attitude of the advisor and faculty members.

TABLE 4. COLLEGE ENVIRONMENT: A COMPARISON OF SATISFACTION WITH THE ATMOSPHERE AND LIVING CONDITIONS BY PERSISTING AND NON-PERSISTING STUDENTS

Items	Persisting N = 201 f	%	Nonpersisting N = 165 f	%	Chi-Square & Probability
Satisfied with atmosphere at school:					
never or seldom = 1	13	6.5	30	18.4	x^2 = 15.1815
sometimes = 2	67	33.3	60	36.8	p = .0005**
most of the time or always = 3	121	60.2	73	44.8	
Satisfied with living conditions:					
= 1	20	10.0	29	17.8	x^2 = 5.2939
= 2	62	31.0	52	31.9	p = .0709
= 3	118	59.0	82	50.3	

** $p < .01$

The data in Table 5 indicated a significant difference in the comparison of the evaluation of the attitudes of the advisors and faculty members by persisting and nonpersisting students. Persisting students reported the attitudes of the advisors and faculty members as more positive than did nonpersisting students.

Approximately the same percentage of persisters in comparison with dropouts indicated a need to talk with their academic advisors. However, a slightly greater percentage of persisting students perceived a need to talk with their faculty members.

Information relevant to the evaluation of the Student Personnel Services by both groups of students is displayed in Table 6. Students responded by checking "below average," "average" or "above average" for any service they used.

The data in Table 6 contain information relevant to the evaluation of the student personnel services by both groups. The Halls of Residence was the only student personnel service found to differ

TABLE 5. COLLEGE ENVIRONMENT: A COMPARISON OF THE NEEDS TO TALK WITH
AND EVALUATION OF THE ATTITUDE OF THE ACADEMIC ADVISORS AND
FACULTY MEMBERS BY PERSISTING AND NONPERSISTING STUDENTS

Items	Persisting N = 201 f	%	Nonpersisting N = 165 f	%	Chi-Square & Probability
Need to talk with academic advisor:					
yes	137	68.5	111	68.1	x^2 = .0010
no	63	31.5	52	31.9	p = .9748
Evaluation of attitude of advisor:					
unconcerned = 1	15	10.7	27	23.9	x^2 = 7.8454
slightly concerned = 2	42	30.0	29	25.7	p = .0198*
concerned = 3	83	59.3	57	50.4	
Need to talk with faculty members:					
yes	164	82.0	125	76.7	x^2 = 1.2517
no	36	18.0	38	23.3	p = .2632
Evaluation of attitude of faculty members:					
= 1	5	3.1	20	16.1	x^2 = 15.1312
= 2	49	30.4	36	29.0	p = .0005**
= 3	107	66.5	68	54.8	

*p < .05
**p < .01

significantly between persisting and nonpersisting students. The persisting students found the Halls of Residence more satisfactory than did nonpersisting students. Even though there was not a significant difference, the Counseling and Psychological Services Center received a greater percentage of "below average" ratings from persisting students than did any other of the student personnel services while this service received the largest percentage of "above average" ratings from the nonpersisting students.

Information relevant to the educational plans of persisting and nonpersisting students is located in Table 7. Students responded by

TABLE 6. COLLEGE ENVIRONMENT: USE AND EVALUATION OF STUDENT PERSONNEL SERVICES BY PERSISTING AND NONPERSISTING STUDENTS

Items	Persisting N = 201 f	%	Nonpersisting N = 165 f	%	Chi-Square & Probability
Academic Advising:					
below average = 1	38	26.4	48	38.7	X^2 = 4.6651
average = 2	77	53.5	56	45.2	p = .0970
above average = 3	29	20.1	20	16.1	
Counseling/Psychological Service Center:					
= 1	9	34.6	13	25.5	X^2 = 1.0530
= 2	10	38.5	9	27.3	p = .5907
= 3	7	26.9	19	37.3	
Dean of Students Office:					
= 1	10	25.0	12	26.1	X^2 = .1496
= 2	19	47.5	20	43.5	p = .9279
= 3	11	27.5	14	30.4	
Halls of Residence:					
= 1	32	20.9	34	32.1	X^2 = 8.2803
= 2	94	61.4	46	43.4	p = .0159*
= 3	27	17.6	26	24.5	
Placement Office:					
= 1	6	13.0	10	30.3	X^2 = 4.8632
= 2	30	65.2	14	42.4	p = .0879
= 3	10	21.7	9	27.3	
University Division Office:					
= 1	16	20.3	13	16.0	X^2 = 1.2437
= 2	47	59.5	46	56.8	p = .5370
= 3	16	20.3	22	27.2	
Reading and Study Skills Center:					
= 1	5	23.8	5	23.8	X^2 = 0.0000
= 2	11	52.4	11	52.4	p = 1.0000
= 3	5	23.8	5	23.8	
Registrar's Office:					
= 1	20	23.3	29	30.2	X^2 = 1.4206
= 2	51	59.3	49	51.0	p = .4915
= 3	15	17.4	18	18.8	
Student Health Center:					
= 1	29	17.9	25	21.2	X^2 = .5286
= 2	78	48.1	56	47.5	p = .7677
= 3	55	34.0	37	31.4	
Scholarship/Financial Aid:					
= 1	29	30.2	30	38.5	X^2 = 1.9450
= 2	48	50.0	31	39.7	p = .3781
= 3	19	19.8	17	21.8	
Other Services:					
= 1	8	38.1	3	33.3	X^2 = .7328
= 2	4	19.0	3	33.3	p = .6932
= 3	9	42.9	3	33.3	

*p < .05

checking being "certain and decided upon," "partially knowing" or being "uncertain and undecided" about their educational goals.

TABLE 7. ACADEMIC CHARACTERISTICS: A COMPARISON OF EDUCATIONAL PLANS UPON ENTERING COLLEGE BETWEEN PERSISTING AND NONPERSISTING STUDENTS

Items	Persisting N = 201 f	%	Nonpersisting N = 165 f	%	Chi - Square & Probability
Plans about educational program were:					
certain and decided	84	42.2	37	22.4	$X^2 = 30.8352$
partially known	86	43.2	65	39.4	$p = .0000**$
uncertain and undecided	29	14.6	63	38.2	

** $p < .01$

The data in Table 7 indicated a significant difference between persisting and nonpersisting students regarding plans about their educational program upon entering college. More persisters expressed being "certain and decided upon" their educational program in comparison to dropouts.

Data relevant to the academic characteristics of the persisting and nonpersisting students are presented in Table 8. Students responded by circling "never or seldom," "sometimes" or "most of the time or always" for each item.

The data in Table 8 indicated there was a statistically significant difference in the responses of persisting and nonpersisting students regarding all academic characteristics. The persisting students expressed a more adequate preparation in their basic academic skills than did the nonpersisting students. The dropouts indicated a greater use of poor study habits, tended to refrain from participation in class discussions, expressed a greater disinterest in their school work and utilized the library less than persisting students.

Information related to the personal characteristics of the persist-

TABLE 8. ACADEMIC CHARACTERISTICS: A COMPARISON BETWEEN PERSISTING AND NONPERSISTING STUDENTS

Items	Persisting N = 201 f	%	Nonpersisting N = 165 f	%	Chi-Square & Probability
Lack basic academic skills:					
never or seldom = 1	133	67.2	88	53.7	x^2 = 7.2353
sometimes = 2	58	29.3	70	42.7	p = .0268*
most of time/always = 3	7	3.5	6	3.7	
Use poor study habits:					
= 1	73	36.3	42	25.6	x^2 = 9.9975
= 2	104	51.7	85	51.2	p = .0067**
= 3	24	11.9	38	23.2	
Participate in class discussions:					
= 1	19	9.5	32	19.5	x^2 = 12.4340
= 2	112	55.7	97	59.1	p = .0020**
= 3	70	34.8	35	21.3	
Interest in school work:					
= 1	11	5.5	18	10.9	x^2 = 20.5930
= 2	67	33.3	85	51.5	p = .0000**
= 3	123	61.2	62	37.6	
Class attendance:					
= 1	8	4.0	6	3.7	x^2 = 24.6813
= 2	20	10.0	50	30.5	p = .0000**
= 3	173	86.1	108	65.9	
Use of library:					
= 1	45	22.4	57	34.8	x^2 = 10.1085
= 2	82	40.8	44	26.8	p = .0064**
= 3	74	36.8	63	38.4	

*p<.05
**p<.01

ing and nonpersisting students is displayed in Table 9A and 9B. Students responded by checking "never or seldom," "sometimes" or "most of the time or always" regarding their concept of the individual characteristics.

Table 9A contains data related to the personal characteristics of the students. Three items were found to differentiate significantly the persisting from the nonpersisting students. These were becoming discouraged with college, being happy in college, and having problems and pressures from parents. The nonpersisters indicated

TABLE 9 A . PERSONAL CHARACTERISTICS: A COMPARISON BETWEEN PERSISTING AND NONPERSISTING STUDENTS

Items	Persisting N = 201 f	%	Nonpersisting N = 165 f	%	Chi-Square & Probability
Became discouraged:					
never or seldom = 1	34	16.9	27	16.4	$x^2 = 19.0131$
sometimes = 2	151	75.1	98	59.4	p = .0001**
most of time/always=3	16	8.0	40	24.2	
Happy in college:					
= 1	3	1.5	24	14.6	$x^2 = 38.8465$
= 2	76	27.8	85	51.8	p = .0000**
= 3	122	60.7	55	33.5	
Felt timid or shy:					
= 1	75	37.3	68	41.5	$x^2 = 4.6607$
= 2	109	54.2	73	44.5	p = .0973
= 3	17	8.5	23	14.0	
Resented authority:					
= 1	100	49.8	98	59.8	$x^2 = 4.6111$
= 2	87	43.3	53	32.3	p = .0997
= 3	14	7.0	13	7.9	
Lacked self-confidence:					
= 1	68	34.0	54	32.9	$x^2 = 5.3899$
= 2	109	54.5	77	47.0	p = .1960
= 3	23	11.5	33	20.1	
Experienced social problems:					
= 1	99	49.3	93	57.8	$x^2 = 3.2590$
= 2	90	44.8	57	35.4	p = .1960
= 3	12	6.0	11	6.8	
Got along with other students:					
= 1	5	2.5	6	3.7	$x^2 = 1.9849$
= 2	17	8.5	20	12.3	p = .3707
= 3	178	89.0	136	84.0	
Had problems/pressures from parents:					
= 1	152	75.6	100	61.7	$x^2 = 14.0501$
= 2	44	29.1	44	27.2	p = .0009**
= 3	5	2.5	18	11.1	

**p <.01

that they were discouraged more frequently with college, were less happy and had more home problems than was indicated by the persisting students. More persisters than dropouts indicated that they "sometimes" resented authority. A slightly greater percentage of the persisting students responded that they "sometimes" lacked self-confidence while more nonpersisting students responded that they lacked self-confidence "most of the time or always." Both groups expressed very little difficulty in getting along with other students. A slightly greater percentage of nonpersisting students indicated feeling timid or shy in comparison with the persisting students.

Information related to the use of alcoholic beverages and non-prescription drugs is displayed in Table 9B. Students responded by checking the frequency of their use of alcoholic beverages and drugs.

TABLE 9 B. PERSONAL CHARACTERISTICS: USE OF ALCOHOLIC BEVERAGES AND NON-PRESCRIPTION DRUGS BY PERSISTING AND NONPERSISTING STUDENTS

Items	Persisting N = 201 f	%	Nonpersisting N = 165 f	%	Chi-Square & Probability
Drink alcoholic beverages:					
never	17	8.5	24	14.7	X^2 = 6.6882
once or twice during semester	54	26.9	42	25.8	p = .0825
once or twice a month	81	40.3	49	30.1	
once or twice a week or more frequently	49	24.4	48	29.4	
Use non-prescription drugs:					
never	106	52.7	82	50.3	X^2 = 4.2224
once or twice during semester	31	15.4	19	11.7	p = .2384
once or twice a month	31	15.4	22	13.5	
once or twice a week or more frequently	33	16.4	40	24.5	

The data in Table 9B contain the frequency of use of alcoholic beverages and nonprescription drugs (marijuana, LSD, etc.) by each group. A slightly greater percentage of dropouts refrained from using alcoholic beverages during the semester.

In close agreement with an earlier drug study at this Midwestern university, approximately half of the students admitted using nonprescription drugs.[1] Several respondents specifically noted on the questionnaire their using marijuana. It appeared that more of the nonpersisters were frequent drug users.

The data in Table 10 contain the reactions of the students toward the purposes of higher education and their perceived practice at the university. The items are arranged in a decreasing order of significance. A statistically significant difference was found between the two groups in four items. The items were: (1) to help a student develop intelligent career plans, (2) to help a student become a well rounded person, (3) to help a student develop better judgment, and (4) to help a student to learn as much as possible about an academic subject area. The interpretations of the four significant items are found in the significant chi-square section.

From Table 10, the item that concerned itself with helping students become psychologically more healthy as a purpose of higher education closely approached a level of significance. More of the dropouts reported a purpose of higher education should be concerned with helping them to become more spontaneous and expressive. It appeared that more persisting students believed a purpose of higher education was to help them become more creative. Persisting and nonpersisting students expressed a slight difference in perceiving two purposes of higher education which were to help students develop a sense of trust, as well as greater capacity for friendlier relationships with others. Both groups indicated they were in agreement that a purpose of higher education was to help them develop independence. To help students become more important and feel more important as a purpose of higher education was perceived by students in both groups as not being practiced.

Information regarding the specific reasons for withdrawing

TABLE 10. PERSONAL AND ACADEMIC CHARACTERISTICS: A COMPARISON OF THE PURPOSES OF HIGHER EDUCATION AND THEIR PRACTICE AT INDIANA UNIVERSITY AS PERCEIVED BY PERSISTING AND NONPERSISTING STUDENTS

Items	Persisting N = 201 f	%	Nonpersisting N = 165 f	%	Chi-Square & Probability
To help us grow and develop as human beings:					
never or seldom = 1	30	14.9	38	23.5	X^2 = 4.4512
sometimes = 2	119	59.2	89	54.9	p = .1080
most of the time or always = 3	52	25.9	35	21.6	
To help us develop independence (be self-sufficient):					
= 1	27	13.4	25	15.3	X^2 = 1.1070
= 2	86	42.8	61	37.4	p = .5749
= 3	88	43.8	77	47.2	
To help us become more spontaneous/expressive:					
= 1	62	30.8	45	27.8	X^2 = 3.7907
= 2	107	53.2	78	48.1	p = .1503
= 3	32	15.9	37	24.1	
To help us become more creative (broaden our interests)					
= 1	44	21.9	40	24.7	X^2 = 1.7091
= 2	113	56.2	80	49.4	p = .4255
= 3	44	21.9	42	25.9	
To help us develop intelligent career plans:					
= 1	40	19.9	62	38.0	X^2 = 19.4296
= 2	98	48.8	75	46.0	p = .0001**
= 3	63	31.3	26	16.0	
To help us develop a sense of trust:					
= 1	71	35.9	65	40.6	X^2 = 2.2196
= 2	102	51.5	82	51.3	p = .3296
= 3	25	12.6	13	8.1	
To help us become well-rounded persons:					
= 1	35	17.4	47	28.8	X^2 = 7.3327
= 2	105	52.2	68	41.7	p = .0256*
= 3	61	30.3	48	29.4	
To help us develop greater capacity for friendly relationships:					
= 1	42	21.0	31	19.6	X^2 = .1528
= 2	95	47.5	78	49.4	p = .9265
= 3	63	31.5	49	31.0	

TABLE 10. (continued)

Items	Persisting N = 201 f	%	Nonpersisting N = 165 f	%	Chi-Square & Probability
To help us be healthier psychologically:					
never or seldom = 1	65	32.7	72	44.4	$x^2 = 5.7533$
sometimes = 2	101	50.8	64	39.5	$p = .0563$
Most of the time or always = 3	33	16.6	26	16.0	
To help us become and feel more important:					
= 1	84	41.8	81	49.7	$x^2 = 2.6804$
= 2	93	46.3	62	38.0	$p = .2618$
= 3	24	11.9	20	12.3	
To help us develop better judgment:					
= 1	27	13.4	48	29.6	$x^2 = 15.5329$
= 2	128	63.7	77	47.5	$p = .0004**$
= 3	46	22.9	37	22.8	
To help us learn as much as possible about an academic subject area:					
= 1	11	5.5	19	11.8	$x^2 = 7.0146$
= 2	97	48.5	85	52.8	$p = .0300*$
= 3	92	46.0	57	35.4	

*$p < .05$
**$p < .01$

from the university by nonpersisting students is presented in Table 11. Nonpersisting students responded by checking any items associated with their decision to withdraw.

The data in Table 11 indicated the specific reasons identified by dropouts for withdrawing from the university. The two most influential factors were dissatisfaction with the general atmosphere and environment at school and financial difficulty. Health problems also played an important role in the decision to withdraw. Reasons not specifically listed but mentioned fre-

TABLE 11. SPECIFIC REASONS FOR WIGHDRAWING FROM SCHOOL BY NONPERSISTING STUDENTS

Items	Nonpersisting Students N = 165	
	f	%
Financial difficulties	44	26.6
Marriage	18	10.9
Health problems	29	17.5
Failure to make good grades	15	9.0
Decided on career not requiring college education	13	7.8
Disliked certain teachers	10	6.0
Joined U.S. Armed Services	2	1.2
Problems with other students	4	2.4
Dissatisfied with general atmosphere/environment of school	73	44.2
Other reasons	82	49.6

quently by the nonpersisting students were general dissatisfaction with academic program and conflict of work with studies. Several of the lowerclassmen expressed a need for a period of time to resolve inner conflicts.

Information related to the decision to transfer to another school is presented in Table 12. Nonpersisting students responded by checking the reasons for transfer or solicited other reasons for transferring to another school.

The data in Table 12 are concerned more specifically with those students who withdrew and transferred to another college as well as the factors influencing them to transfer. A minority of those who withdrew reported that they actually transferred to continue their education.

In review of the responses given, no one reason dominated the decision to transfer. Reasons indicated by the transferees for leaving were a desire for a smaller school environment, a better quality program and unavailability of specific programs at the university.

TABLE 12. FACTORS INFLUENCING THE DECISION TO WITHDRAW AND/OR TRANSFER BY NONPERSISTING STUDENTS

Item	Nonpersisting Students N = 165 f	%
Transferred to another college:		
yes	42	28.3
no	106	71.6
Transferred because:		
less expensive at other school	6	13.6
school closer to home	8	18.1
other reasons	30	68.1

Significant Chi-Squares

As mentioned in the preceding section, this section deals with the presentation and interpretation of items found significant below the .05 level.

The data in Table 13 contain information related to significant home environmental characteristics.

Three items generated a significant chi-square for the home environmental factors. The items related to father's educational level, health or medical problems and personal problems at home. It was observed that a majority of the fathers of the dropouts had not entered college. On the other hand, a majority of the fathers of the persisting students had completed 2 years of college or more. A significant difference was also found between the persisting and nonpersisting students with a greater percentage of the dropouts having health or medical problems and personal problems.

Information relevant to significant college environmental characteristics is displayed in Table 14 and 15. Table 14 contains information related to the degree of the student's satisfaction with

TABLE 13. HOME ENVIRONMENT: FATHER'S EDUCATION/PROBLEMS AT HOME

Items	Persisting N = 201 %N	Nonpersisting N = 165 %N	Chi-Square & Probability
Father's educational level:			
high school or lower	34.8	53.9	$x^2 = 19.2310$
up to 2 years of college	9.0	8.5	$p = .0007**$
up to Bachelor's degree	31.8	27.3	
up to Master's degree	14.9	7.9	
Doctorate or equivalent	9.5	2.4	
Problems at home:			
health or medical	6.0	13.9	$x^2 = 5.6897$ $p = .0171*$
personal	22.5	33.3	$x^2 = 4.8037$ $p = .0284*$

$*p < .05$
$**p < .01$

the atmosphere at school and the evaluation of the attitudes of the academic advisor and faculty members.

The data in Table 14 indicated a significant chi-square for three college environmental factors. It was found that a majority of the dropouts were satisfied with the general atmosphere at school only sometimes or never; however, a greater majority of the persisting students expressed satisfaction with the general atmosphere "most of the time or always." The data also indicated that a far greater percentage of the nonpersisting students perceived the attitudes of their advisors to be one of unconcern. It was also observed that a greater percentage of the persisting students perceived the attitudes of their advisors to be concerned. Similarly, a far greater percentage of the dropouts believed the attitudes of their faculty members to be unconcerned.

The data in Table 15 include the evaluation of the student

TABLE 14. COLLEGE ENVIRONMENT: SATISFACTION WITH ATMOSPHERE AND AN EVALUATION OF ATTITUDES

Items	Persisting N = 201 % N	Nonpersisting N = 165 % N	Chi-Square & Probability
Satisfied with atmosphere at school:			
never or seldom = 1	6.5	18.4	x^2 = 15.1815
sometimes = 2	33.3	36.8	p = .0005**
most of time or always = 3	60.2	44.8	
Evaluation/attitude of advisor:			
unconcerned = 1	10.7	23.9	x^2 = 7.8454
slightly concerned = 2	30.0	25.7	p = .0198*
concerned = 3	59.3	50.4	
Evaluation/attitude of faculty members:			
unconcerned = 1	3.5	16.1	x^2 = 15.1312
slightly concerned = 2	30.4	29.0	p = .0005**
concerned = 3	66.5	54.8	

*p < .05
**p < .01

personnel service found to be significant. Students responded by checking "below average," "average" or "above average."

The data in Table 15 indicated a greater majority of the persisting students than nonpersisting students to have evaluated the Halls of Residence to be average and above average. It was also disclosed that a greater percentage of the nonpersisting students than persisting students evaluated the service to be below average.

Information concerning the students' degree of certainty about their educational program is located in Table 16. Students responded by checking being "certain and decided," "partially knowing" or being "uncertain and undecided" about their educational goals.

TABLE 15. COLLEGE ENVIRONMENT: STUDENT PERSONNEL SERVICE

Item	Persisting N = 201 % N	Nonpersisting N = 165 % N	Chi-Square & Probability
Halls of Residence:			
below average = 1	20.9	32.1	X^2 = 8.2803
average = 2	61.4	43.4	p = .0159*
above average = 3	17.6	24.5	

*p < .05

The data in Table 16 revealed a significant difference between persisting and nonpersisting students regarding plans about their educational program. It was found that a far greater percentage of persisters than dropouts were certain and decided about their educational goals upon entering college. On the other hand, a far

TABLE 16. ACADEMIC CHARACTERISTICS: EDUCATIONAL PROGRAM

Item	Persisting N = 201 % N	Nonpersisting N = 165 % N	Chi-Square & Probability
Plans about educational program:			
certain and decided = 1	42.2	22.4	X^2 = 30.8352
partially known = 2	43.2	39.4	p = .0000*
uncertain and undecided = 3	14.6	38.4	

**p < .01

TABLE 17. ACADEMIC CHARACTERISTICS: BASIC SKILLS, STUDY HABITS AND
INTEREST, CLASS PARTICIPATION AND ATTENDANCE, LIBRARY USE

Items	Persisting N = 201 % N	Nonpersisting N = 165 % N	Chi-Square & Probability
Lacked basic academic skills:			
never or seldom = 1	67.2	53.7	X^2 = 7.2353
sometimes = 2	29.3	42.7	p = .0268*
most of the time or always = 3	3.5	3.7	
Used poor study habits: = 1	36.3	35.6	X^2 = 9.9975
= 2	51.7	51.2	p = .0067**
= 3	11.9	23.2	
Participated in class			
discussions: = 1	9.5	19.5	X^2 = 12.4340
= 2	55.7	59.1	p = .0020**
= 3	34.8	21.3	
Interested in school work:			
= 1	5.5	10.9	X^2 = 20.5930
= 2	33.3	51.5	p = .0000**
= 3	61.2	37.6	
Class attendance:			
= 1	4.0	3.7	X^2 = 24.6813
= 2	10.0	30.5	p = .0000**
= 3	86.1	65.9	
Use of library:			
never or once or twice = 1	22.4	34.8	X^2 = 10.1085
once or twice a month = 2	40.8	26.8	p = .0064**
about 2 hours a week or more frequently = 3	36.8	38.4	

*p < .05
**p < .01

greater percentage of nonpersisting students than persisting students indicated that they were uncertain and undecided about their educational goals upon entering college.

Information relevant to significant academic factors is displayed in Table 17. Students responded by circling "never or seldom," "sometimes" or "most of the time or always" for each item. The data in Table 17 found six significant academic characteristics between persisting and nonpersisting students. More of the persisters than dropouts responded as having adequate academic skills. A greater percentage of the dropouts stated that they used poor study habits most of the time or always while a larger percentage of persisting students stated that they seldom or never used poor study habits. Persisting students were found to participate more frequently in class discussion than did dropouts. A far greater percentage of persisting than nonpersisting students indicated "most of the time or always" being interested in school work and attending classes. Finally, a greater percentage of dropouts indicated either no use of the library or use of the library once or twice during the semester.

Information regarding the three significant personal characteristics of the persisting and nonpersisting students is displayed in Table 18. Students responded by checking "never or seldom," "sometimes" or "most of the time or always" regarding their concept of the individual characteristics.

The data in Table 18 described a greater percentage of the dropouts to be discouraged more frequently than persisting students. A far greater percentage of persisters were found to be happy in college most of the time or always. Finally, it was indicated that a greater majority of the persisting students had fewer problems and pressures from parents.

Information related to the four significant purposes of higher education and their perceived practice at this Midwestern university by the two groups is presented in Table 19. Students responded by checking how frequently they perceived these purposes to be practiced at the university.

TABLE 18.   PERSONAL CHARACTERISTICS: DISCOURAGEMENT, HAPPINESS AND PARENTAL PRESSURES

Items	Persisting N = 201 % N	Nonpersisting N = 165 % N	Chi-Square & Probability
Became discouraged:			
never or seldom = 1	16.9	16.4	$X^2 = 19.0131$
sometimes = 2	75.1	59.4	$p = .0001**$
most of time/always = 3	8.0	24.2	
Happy with college:			
= 1	1.5	14.6	$X^2 = 38.8465$
= 2	37.8	51.8	$p = .0000**$
= 3	60.7	33.5	
Had problems with and pressure from parents:			
= 1	75.6	61.7	$X^2 = 14.0501$
= 2	29.1	27.2	$p = .0009**$
= 3	2.5	11.1	

**p < .01

The data in Table 19 indicated four significant items regarding the purposes of higher education and their perceived practice at the university. The items related to developing intelligent career plans, becoming a well rounded person, developing better judgment and learning as much as possible about an academic subject area. A significant difference was found between persisting and nonpersisting students. A greater percentage of nonpersisting students believed the university was unsuccessful in helping students to develop intelligent career plans and helping them to learn as much as possible about an academic subject area. Also, more nonpersisting students felt the university was unsuccessful in helping students to develop better judgment and to become well rounded individuals.

[1]Crowe, J., *et. al.*, *Indiana University Drug Study*, op. cit., p. 68.

TABLE 19. PERSONAL AND ACADEMIC CHARACTERISTICS: CAREER PLANS, BECOMING WELL-ROUNDED, DEVELOPING JUDGMENT, LEARNING SUBJECT AREA

Items	Persisting N = 201 % N	Nonpersisting N = 165 % N	Chi-Square & Probability
To help us develop intelligent career plans:			
never or seldom = 1	19.9	38.0	$X^2 = 19.4296$
sometimes = 2	48.8	46.0	$p = .0001**$
most of time/always = 3	31.3	16.0	
To help us become well-rounded:			
= 1	17.4	28.8	$X^2 = 7.3327$
= 2	52.2	41.7	$p = .0256*$
= 3	30.3	29.4	
To help us develop better judgment:			
= 1	13.4	29.6	$X^2 = 15.5329$
= 2	63.7	47.5	$p = .0004**$
= 3	22.9	22.8	
Ro help us learn as much as possible about academic subject matter:			
= 1	5.5	11.8	$X^2 = 7.0146$
= 2	48.5	52.8	$p = .0300*$
= 3	46.0	35.4	

*p < .05
**p < .01

Chapter IV

SUMMARY, CONCLUSIONS, RECOMMENDATIONS, EPILOGUE AND COMMENTS

The purpose of Chapter IV is fourfold: (1) to present a general summary of the background and procedures of the present investigation; (2) to present the findings and conclusions of the study; (3) to present the recommendations based on the conclusions of the study and to suggest avenues of further research related to this topic, and (4) to close with a general discussion of the problem.

Summary of Background and Procedures

The school dropout problem has been a national as well as an international concern at all levels of education. The dropout problem is not a new phenomenon. As early as 1872 the problem of dropouts was discussed at the annual convention of the National Education Association.

A review of the literature indicated that the average retention of the nation's colleges and universities was as follows: approximately 40 percent complete a bachelor's degree within four years, another 20 percent graduate in succeeding years, and approximately 40 percent fail to graduate at all. Data at the national level found a variety of reasons for students' dropping out of college. Students withdraw for academic, personal, financial, environmental or psychological reasons. The data revealed students seldom leave for a single reason.

Past research at this university has been primarily concerned with either persisting or nonpersisting students. These studies generally were concerned with such factors as perceptions of entering freshmen, comparison of students attending three different colleges, influences of environment upon grades, study of body types in freshmen females, attitudes of undergraduates and a general study on dropouts which was completed in 1953.

Very little specific and up-to-date information was available about nonpersisting students at this university. Data also were not available regarding a comparison of persisting and nonpersisting students. Thus, it appeared that other studies concerned with the dropout problem at this university were needed. The present study examined the responses of a sample of persisting and nonpersisting students with regards to their home environment, their college environment, and their personal, emotional and academic characteristics. Specifically, the purpose of this study was to identify and contrast the differences in responses to a number of questionnaire items related to interests, feelings, needs, goals and personal and academic problems between persisting and nonpersisting students.

Methods and Procedures

A survey form of research was adopted to obtain this information. The general procedure in this study involved selecting two random samples consisting of 250 persisting and 250 nonpersisting students. The names, addresses and descriptive data were academic advising, (5) Counseling and Psychological Service Center, (6) Dean of Students Office, (7) Placement Office, (8) University Division Office, (9) Reading and Study Skills Center, (10) Registrar's Office, (11) Student Health Center, (12) Scholarship and Financial Aids, and (13) other services.

Regarding the null hypothesis, there was no significant difference between the personal, emotional, and academic characteristics of persisting and nonpersisting students. There were twenty-nine items within this cluster. Fourteen items were rejected and fifteen items were accepted. The fourteen significant personal and academic characteristics were: (1) plans about educational goals, .01 level; (2) use of poor study habits, .01 level; (3) participation in class discussions, .01 level; (4) interest in school work, .01 level; (5) class attendance, .01 level; (6) use of library, .01 level; (7) lack of basic academic skills, .05 level; (8) becoming discouraged, .01 level; (9) happy in college, .01 level; (10) parental pressures and problems, .01 level; (11) to help us develop intelligent career plans, .01 level; (12) to help us develop better judgment, .01 level; (13) to help us become a well rounded person, .05 level, and (14) to help us to learn as much as possible about an academic subject area, .05 level.

The fifteen insignificant personal, emotional and academic characteristics were: (1) felt timid or shy, (2) resented authority, (3) lacked self-confidence, (4) experienced social problems, (5) got along with other students, (6) drank alcoholic beverages, (7) used nonprescription drugs, (8) to help us grow and develop as human beings, (9) to help us develop independence (be self-sufficient), (10) to help us become more spontaneous and expressive, (11) to help us become more creative (broaden our interests), (12) to help us develop a sense of trust, (13) to help us develop a greater capacity for friendlier relationships with others, (14) to help us become psychologically more healthy, and (15) to help us become and feel more important.

Conclusions

The results of the present study appear to warrant the following conclusions based on the analysis of data relative to persisting and nonpersisting students from the 1973 fall semester at a major university.

1. The evidence suggested that it is unlikely that a student with academic disabilities and personal pressures will continue his education.
2. Students with academic and personal problems can be identified as potential dropouts.
3. A father's educational level is highly indicative of whether a student will persist or withdraw.
4. A positive personal relationship with a student's advisor and faculty members influences his chances to remain in school.
5. The evidence suggested that the needs of the students have not been adequately satisfied by the student personnel services.
6. The evidence suggested that a sufficient number of programs and courses were available to students at the university.
7. One can speculate that having a definite educational goal in mind enhances persistence in college.
8. The dropout problem suggests that something is wrong with our educational institutions. Apparently current educational practices are treating a symptom and not the real cause of the problem.
9. The university needs to continue to explore ways of not only keeping students in college until they complete their degrees, but also of giving them a useful and meaningful education.

Recommendations

The following recommendations have been developed with the expressed purpose of suggesting programmatic guidelines for the university in order to help curtail the college dropout problem.

1. The university should seek improved procedures to help students who come to college with academic, personal and home problems since, such problems are often the underlying cause of students' withdrawing prematurely from college. The university must provide more effective personal counseling conjoint with other student personnel services.

2. A careful evaluation of students' background characteristics and level of study skills by related student personnel services should be made with an emphasis on identifying potential dropouts before they become dropouts. This information should be shared with related faculty members.

3. Since a greater percentage of persisting students was found to have concrete educational goals, improved and innovative career and vocational counseling should become a priority of the university. Students will then be afforded a more meaningful educational experience if they are assisted in making an intelligent choice of a career which is compatible with their interests, strengths, goals and personality.

4. Improved academic guidance for students on the part of university personnel appears to be warranted. A suggested approach could be the use of competent upperclassmen to act as turors and advisors for students who are experiencing difficulty in academic areas. The university could take the responsibility to coordinate interclass peer tutoring programs.

5. Informal drop-in centers should be established throughout the campus, where students could receive academic assistance whenever needed.

6. Based upon the fact that a high percent of nonpersisting students indicated having difficulty in academic preparation for college, such programs as are found at the Reading and Study Skills Center should be enthusiastically supported by the univer-

sity. In addition, this service should include other academic skills and assistance. Students with marginal academic preparation should be encouraged to attend remedial programs in academic areas at the university during the summer before entering college as well as during their entire residence on campus.

7. University faculty should be selected not only for their ability to teach but also for the capability to act as effective student advisors. Of the existing faculty members, only those who are capable and want to work with students as advisors should be appointed to do so.

8. An improved and expanded orientation program should be developed for faculty and advisors concerning the psychodynamics of student behavior and its relationship to persistence in college. Too few college and university personnel are aware of the seriousness of their roles in assisting students to stay and graduate from college.

9. Students identified as potential dropouts should be involved in special orientation activities. For example, special group counseling should be initiated for students identified as potential nonpersisters.

10. A continuous evaluation of student personnel services is extremely necessary in order to ensure that the services provided are meeting the needs of the students as well as the objectives of the institution. Too much specialization and compartmentalization of services tends to loose its effectiveness with such students as identified in this study.

A follow-up study should be made on nonpersisting students to determine the differences between those students who return and those who do not return. Other studies should be undertaken to evaluate the effects of remedial summer programs on students who participate in such programs prior to their first semester in college, the influence of peer tutoring and its effects on students' grade point averages, and the differences in persisting and nonpersisting students over a period of several years.

Epilogue

Although a large number of students drop out of college and universities annually, it appears that many of them could be retained and salvaged. By becoming more sensitive to the needs and differences of students, especially those who exhibit some form of personal, social and/or academic distress, it is entirely possible that institutions of higher education could decelerate the current army of potential college dropouts festering on campuses throughout the United States and awaiting their time to withdraw.

Even in these times when *in loco parentis* is becoming a discredited principle and talk of complete student freedom is in vogue, it seems apparent that the university must continue to guide the academic and personal development of all students. These age old university-student problems persist: parental pressures and problems; dissatisfaction with the general atmosphere at school; poor student-faculty relationships; disinterest in school; lack of basic academic skills; discouragement and unhappiness, and perception of the university as failing in its purposes. These findings have obvious implications for deans of student affairs and academic areas, as well as all university personnel. The university must create an improved vigorous mechanism for ongoing student-faculty interaction, as well as work on both the academic and social habits of students, whether they live in residence halls or off campus. Such programs rest primarily on the university since it is often most difficult for students who have problems to carry out successfully a coherent strategy of self-improvement and pursuit of educational goals.

The Impact of the Collegiate Experience on Some Students:
Some Comments
BY
Joseph P. Cangemi
Western Kentucky University

Attending college is a traumatic experience for many students and the literature abounds with data that support this contention. For example, the distance a college or university is from a student's home, the kinds of organizations in which he participates, the professors, other students, specific courses, the curriculum, housing arrangements, etc. all are impacts that are pressed upon a student, influences which require some form of adjustment. Many students are able to handle satisfactorily the emotional aspects of these impacts while others are not and, as a consequence, suffer a great deal of difficulty. Those who do not adjust very well to the impacts created by the college experience usually become discouraged and withdraw.

Research has demonstrated that approximately seventy percent of those who withdraw from their college studies could have profited from the experience. That is, they had the intellectual capacity to complete college level work successfully. The research further has pointed out that many reasons for dropping out are non-academic. The essential reasons are related to problems of a personal, social, religious, emotional, familial, and/or economic nature, problems generally that do have solutions. Those who simply do not have the intellectual capacity to remain at college are unfortunately, in a situation beyond repair. For them, withdrawal should be seen as a healthy form of adjustment, because remaining in college easily could breed unhealthy responses as the student finds himself in failure-type situations far more often than in success-type circumstances.

The seventy percent of college students who quit but who do have the academic and intellectual talent necessary to satisfy degree requirements must be helped to remain in school because, for them, not persisting in college is not only a waste of human talent, it is also a social waste—something no society can afford. Without a degree of some kind, at this time in the United States it is becoming increasingly difficult to secure numerous positions. Today, college degrees are often required for positions that, just a few years back, required only a high school diploma. The college degree opens doors to its holder. When compared with non-degree holders, college degree holders generally receive more rapid advancement, additional training, greater income, more responsibility, and opportunities for specialization and advanced schooling. The degrees seems to suggest to those who are recruiting that the individual who possesses one has more perserverance and endurance, more patience, more ambition, more intelligence, more drive and motivation, etc., than one who has quit his studies. Whether these perceptions are valid or not is a moot point. The facts are that the college degree today is being used more and more as a screening device to provide those with this level of certified accomplishment the type of opportunities that are becoming increasingly difficult to obtain in any other way. For the seventy percent that have the intellectual capacity to grind out their college diplomas, the fact that they do not is suggestive that institutions of higher education have not done all in their power to help students overcome the non-intellectual impediments that persistently cause them to leave their studies rather than persevere with them.

Many nonpersisting college students might have stayed and completed their programs and earned their degrees if only they could have received some encouragement or assistance at a particular, crucial time during their collegiate experience. Unfortunately, many of them apparently received none—or very little. The present emphasis in higher education seems almost totally dedicated to intellectual excellence, discipline pursuit, and grades. Interest in students and their personal and academic problems seems at best to be sporadic, more the result of some humanistically oriented professors than a product of institutional philosophy and policy. The student as human being seems not to be an important concept in far too many institutions of higher education, but rather seems more appreciated as a statistic: a degree aspirant, a major, a minor, a female, a datum to report for state financial support, possessor of a good I.Q., a genius, and a potential member of a discipline, among other things. In short, in too many institutions of higher learning the student is perceived as an entity, a thing, something to feed intellectually and to obtain from in return conditioned, regurgitated feedback, or to use as an appropriate statistic for the benefit of the institution or the state.

Coddling students is not the alternative. The alternative that is suggested to perceiving students impersonally and statistically is to perceive them as sensitive, important human beings engaged in one of the most valuable and profitable experiences of their lives, an experience which, if handled successfully easily could mean the difference between a life of substantial quality as opposed to one of lesser quality. The unsuccessful college experience means the loss of that quality of life that could have been obtained; one that was within grasp. For that seventy percent that had the intellectual ability to perform well enough to earn a college education but who did not, this condemnation to a life of lesser quality is unfortunate.

That nonpersisting college students felt they were treated in ways which were unsatisfactory is seen in the data compiled by Kowalski. Kowalski's research compared persisting and nonpersisting college students and demonstrated that colleges in general, were significantly deficient in helping the latter to develop intelligent career plans and better judgment, in helping them to become better adjusted and well rounded as human beings, and in helping them to become more knowledgeable about a particular area of academic studies. Interestingly, nonpersisting students felt very strongly about these perceived deficiencies, enough perhaps to have had a substantial negative impact on them; enough perhaps also to have had some influence on their decision to leave school.

Higher education is at a time in the course of its history when it must undergo an examination of its goals and purposes. The time has come for a serious evaluation of the purposes for existence of many institutions of higher learning, particularly those where the professors pride themselves on the number of students they manage to flunk out annually. Institutions of education must become dedicated to helping human beings become the best they can possibly become. Until more colleges and universities start perceiving students as having personal, social, and emotional needs, as opposed to just academic needs, not much will be done to stop the flow of young people from leaving college who might have stayed and learned a better education—and a better life.

BIBLIOGRAPHY

Alexander, Ruth H., *A Study Of Body Types, Self-Image And Environmental Adjustment In Freshman College Females*, Unpublished doctor's thesis, School of Education, Indiana University, Bloomington, June, 1967, 128 pp.
Appel, Victor H., and Witzke, Donald B., *Goal Orientation Vs. Self-Orientation: Two Perspectives Affecting Indecision About Collegiate Major And Career Choice*, ERIC, no. ED 063 855, American Educational Research Association Annual Meeting, Chicago, April, 1972, 13 pp.
Astin, Alexander W., *College Dropouts: A National Profile*, ERIC, no. ED 059 691, American Council On Education, Office of Research, Washington, D.C., February, 1972, 78 pp.
Bailey, Benjamin H., *Characteristics of High School Seniors As Related to Subsequent College Attendance*, Cooperative

Research Project No. 21 57, West Virginia University, June, 1966, 85 pp.

Barkey, Patrick, "Patterns of Student Use of a College Library," *College and Research Libraries*, 26:115-118, March, 1965.

Benezet, Louis T., "College Study: Expectations and Realities," pp. 1-21, in *The First Years In College: Preparing Students For A Successful College Career*, edited by Harry N. Rivlin, *et. al.*, Little Brown and Company, Boston, 1965, 605 pp.

Berdie, Ralph H., *Characteristics of Students Today*, ERIC, no. ED 038 090, Minnesota University, Minneapolis, February 10, 1966, 18 pp.

Blaine, Graham B., and McArthur, Charles C., *et. al., Emotional Problems of the Student*, A Doubleday-Anchor Book, New York, 1966, 313 pp.

Borg, Walter R., and Gall, Meredith D., *Educational Research An Introduction*, second edition, David McKay Co., Inc., New York, 1971, 533 pp.

Brown, Robert D., *Student Development in Tomorrow's Higher Education—A Return to the Academy*, American College Personnel Association, Washington, D.C., 1972, 55 pp.

Brown, Robert D., *Parental Perceptions of University Life and Their Characterizations of Their College Sons and Daughters*, ERIC, no. ED 038 699, United States Department of Health, Education and Welfare, Office of Education, 1970, 16 pp.

Bucklin, Robert W., and Bucklin, Mary Lou, *The Psychological Characteristics of the College Persister and Leaver: A Review*, ERIC, no. ED 049 709, August, 1970, 19 pp.

Cangemi, Joseph P., *Perceptions Of Students, Faculty and Administrators Regarding Self-Actualization As the Purpose of Higher Education*, Unpublished doctor's thesis, School of Education, Indiana University, Bloomington, May, 1974, 93 pp.

Cangemi, Joseph P., and Coan, Donald L., "A Clinical Method For Identifying Potential Dropouts," *College Student Journal*, 7:78-82, January-February, 1973.

Centra, John A., "How Students Perceive Their College Environments," *College Board Review*, 79:11-13, Spring, 1971.

Chase, Clinton I., "The College Dropout: His High School Prologue," *Bulletin of the National Association of Secondary School Principals,* 54:66-71, January-May, 1970.

Chase, Clinton I., and Warren, Suzanne, *Freshmen View The College Scene: Opinions Before And After The Initial Semester*, ERIC, no. ED 029 592, Indiana Studies in Prediction, Monograph of the Bureau of Educational Studies and Testing, United States Department of Health, Education and Welfare, Office of Education, 1969, 20 pp.

Chickering, Arthur W., *Institutional Differences And Student Characteristics*, ERIC, no. ED 014 099, Plainfield, Vermont, May, 1966, 19 pp.

Chickering, Arthur W., *Education And Identity*, Jossey-Bass, Inc., Publishers, San Francisco, 1969, 367 pp.

Chickering, Arthur W., and McCormick, John, *Personality Development And The College Experience*, ERIC, no. ED 042 402, Project on Student Development in Small Colleges, National Institute of Mental Health, Bethesda, Maryland, 1970, 45 pp.

Chickering, Arthur W., and Hannah, William, "The Process of Withdrawal," *Liberal Education*, 55:551-558, December, 1969.

Clark, Burton R.; Heist, Paul; McConnell, T. R.; Trow, Martin, A., and Younge, George, *Students and Colleges: Introduction and Change*, Center for Research and Development in Higher Education, University of California, Berkeley, 1972, 327 pp.

Coker, David L., *Diversity Of Intellective And Non-Intellective Characteristics Between Persisting And Non-Persisting Students Among Campuses*, ERIC, no. ED 033 645, Wisconsin State University, Stevens Point, April, 1968, 112 pp.

Cope, Robert G., "Are Students More Likely To Drop Out of Large Colleges," *College Student Journal*, 6:92-97, April-May, 1972.

Cope, Robert G., and Hewitt, Raymond G., *A Typology of College Dropouts: An Environmental Approach*, ERIC, no. ED 030 392, Massachusetts University, Amherst, June, 1969, 26 pp.

Cope, Robert G., et. al., *An Investigation of Entrance Characteristics Related To Types of College Dropouts: Final Report*, ERIC, no. ED 052 749, College of Education, Washington University, Seattle, May, 1971, 261 pp.

Crowe, James W., et. al., *Indiana University Drug Study*, Indiana University, Bloomington, November 22, 1972, 156 pp.

DeCoster, David A., "Effects of Homogeneous Housing Assignments For High Ability Students," *The Journal of College Student Personnel,* 9:75-78, April, 1968.

Dellenback, John, "Report On Proprietary Vocational Schools," *Congressional Record*, Washington, D.C., 116:1-6, August 12, 1970.

Demos, George D., "Analysis of College Dropouts—Some Manifest and Covert Reasons," *Personnel and Guidance Journal*, 46:681-684, March, 1968.

Dollar, Robert J., "Interpersonal Values and College Persistence," *The Journal of College Student Personnel*, 11:200-209, May, 1970.

Duling, John A., "Differences in Perceptions of the Environmental Press by Selected Sub-Groups," *Journal of the National Association of Women Deans and Counselors*, 32:130-132, 1968.

Elton, Charles F., "Personality of Low Income Males: College Versus Non-college," *The Journal of College Student Personnel*, 11:210-212, May, 1970.

Feldman, Kenneth A., and Newcomb, Theodore N., *The Impact*

Of College On Students, Jossey-Bass Inc., Publishers, San Francisco, 1969, 383 pp.

Fox, Ljunberg, "Effecting the Use of Efficient Study Habits," *Journal of Mathematics*, 1:75-86, 1962.

Gelso, Charles J., "Some Findings About Student Study Patterns," *College Student Survey*, 3:49-54, Winter, 1969.

George, Rickey L., "Resident Or Commuter: A Study of Personality Differences," *The Journal of College Student Personnel*, 12:216-219, May, 1971.

George, Rickey L., and Marshall, Jon C., "Personality of Young Adults: College vs. Non-College," *The Journal of College Student Personnel*, 12:438-444, November, 1971.

Gibson, Raymond C., *The Challenge of Leadership In Higher Education*, Wm. C. Brown Company, Publishers, Dubuque, Iowa, 1969, 362 pp.

Gibson, Robert L.; Higgins, Robert and Mitchell, Marianne H., "The High School Dropout Goes To College," *Personnel and Guidance Journal*, 45:824-827, April, 1967.

Goetsch, Helen B., *Parental Income And College Opportunities*, Teachers College Contributions to Education, Number 795, Columbia University Press, Columbia University, New York, 1940, 157 pp.

Greenleaf, Elizabeth Adele, *A Comparison Of Women At Indiana University Majoring In Three Different Colleges*, Unpublished doctor's thesis, School of Education, Indiana University, Bloomington, August, 1952, 168 pp.

Greenshields, Myrel J., "The College Going Decision: High School Seniors Give Their Reasons," *College and University*, 32:208-217, Winter, 1957.

Gurin, G.; Newcomb, Theodore M., and Cope, Robert G., *Characteristics of Entering Freshmen Related to Attrition in the Literary College of a Large State University*, Final Report, University of Michigan, Project Number 1938, United States Office of Education, Washington, D.C., January, 1968.

Gustavus, William T., "Successful Students, Readmitted Students, and Dropouts: A Comparative Study of Student Attrition," *Social Science Quarterly*, 53:136-144, June, 1972.

Hancock, Bruce A., *Undergraduate Student Attitudes And Factors Influencing Attitudes*, Unpublished doctor's thesis, School of Education, Indiana University, Bloomington, June 1971, 117 pp.

Hagen, E.W., *The Sophomore Norming Sample for the General Examinations of the Comprehensive College Tests*, Educational Testing Service, Princeton, New Jersey, 1964.

Hannah, William, "Withdrawal From College," *The Journal of College Student Personnel*, 10:397-402, November, 1969.

Hannah, William, "Personality Differences Between Lower Division Dropouts and Stayins," *The Journal of College Student Personnel*, 12:16-19, January, 1971.

Heath, Douglas H., *Growing Up In College*, Jossey-Bass, Inc., Publishers, San Francisco, 1968, 326 pp.

Hedley, William H., *Freshman Survival And Attrition At A Small, Private Liberal Arts College: A Discriminant Analysis Of Intellectual And Non-Intellectual Variables*, Unpublished doctor's thesis, Washington State University, Ann Arbor, Michigan, University Microfilms, Number 68-10,959, 1968.

Hedlund, Dalva E., and Jones, Terry J., "Effect of Student Personnel Services on Completion Rate In Two-Year Colleges," *The Journal of College Student Personnel*, 11:196-199, May, 1970.

Henry, John L., *Student Characteristics And Perception Of Indiana University*, Unpublished doctor's thesis, School of Education, Indiana University, Bloomington, June, 1966, 170 pp.

Heywood, John, "A Report On Student Wastage," *Universities Quarterly*, 25:189-237, Spring, 1971.

Holland, John L., "Student Explanations of College Choices and Their Relation to College Popularity, College Productivity and Sex Differences," *College and University*, 33:313-320, Spring, 1958.

Hornbostel, Victor O., et. al., *The Rehabilitation of School Dropouts In Oklahoma City:* (An Experimental Appraisal), Ford Foundation, Research Foundation, Oklahoma State University, Stillwater, Oklahoma, 1969, 125 pp.

Huber, William H., "Channeling Students For Greater Retention," *College and University*, 47:19-29, Fall, 1971.

Hughes, Anita L., *Diversity of Characteristics And Judgments of Indiana University's Regional Campus Transfer Students*, Unpublished doctor's thesis, School of Education, Indiana University, Bloomington, September, 1967, 145 pp.

Hummel, Rossi Barbara, *The Development of Intellectual Commitment In University Students*, ERIC, no. ED 063 856, New York University, New York, April, 1972, 24 pp.

Iffert, Robert E., *Retention and Withdrawal of College Students*, Superintendent of Documents, Office of Education, Government Printing Office, Washington, D.C., 1958, 177 pp.

Iffert, Robert E., and Clarke, Betty S., *College Applicants, Entrants, Dropouts*, ERIC, no. ED 055 560, United States Department of Health, Education and Welfare, Office of Education, Washington, D.C., 1965, 96 pp.

Ikenberry, Stanley O., "Factors in College Persistence," *Journal of Counseling Psychology*, 8:322-329, Winter, 1961.

Jennings, Jerry T., *Undergraduate Enrollment In Two-Year and Four-Year Colleges*, ERIC, no. ED 067 971, Superintendent of Documents, United States Government Printing Office, Washington, D.C., June, 1972, 27 pp.

Joff, A. and Adams, W., "Open Admissions and Academic Quality," *Change*, 3:11, March-April, 1971.

Johnston, Sylvia, *A Comparison of Environmental Perceptions of Student Subgroups In Residence Halls*, ERIC, no. ED 053

667, Missouri University, Columbia, December, 1971, 20 pp.

Jones, Gordon and Dennison, John D., *A Comparative Study of Persister and Non-Persister College Students*, ERIC, no. ED 062 975, Vancouver City College, British Columbia, June, 1972, 100 pp.

Kamens, David H., "The College Charter And College Size: Factors On Occupational Choice And College Attrition," *Sociology of Education*, 44:270-296, Summer, 1971.

Kapur, Robert L., "Student Wastage At Edinburgh University: Factors Related To Failure And Dropout," *Universities Quarterly*, 26:353-377, Summer, 1972.

Katz, Joseph and Sanford, Nevitt, "Curriculum and Personality," pp. 121-132, in *College and Character*, edited by Nevitt Sanford, Wiley, New York, New York, 1964, 308 pp.

Kerlinger, Fred N., *Foundations of Behavioral Research*, Holt, Rinehart and Winston, Inc., New York, 1964, 739 pp.

Knoell, Dorothy N., "A Critical Review of Research on the College Dropout," pp. 63-81 in *The College Dropout And The Utilization of Talent*, by Lawrence A. Pervin, Louis E. Reik, and Willard Dalrymple, Princeton University Press, Princeton, New Jersey, 1966, 260 pp.

Koelsche, Charles L., *A Study Of The Student Drop-Out Problem At Indiana University*, Unpublished doctor's thesis, School of Education, Indiana University, Bloomington, August, 1953, 164 pp.

Kojaku, Lawrence K., *Major Field Transfer: The Self-Matching Of University Undergraduates To Student Characteristics*, ERIC, no. ED 062 933, California University, Los Angeles, 1971, 6 pp.

Kooker, Earl W., and Bellamy, Roy Q., "Some Psychometric Differences Between Graduates and Dropouts," *Psychology: A Journal of Human Behavior*, 6:65-70, May, 1969.

Kowalski, Casimir J., and Cangemi, Joseph P., "High School

Dropouts: A Lost Resource," *College Student Journal*, 8: 71-74, November-December, 1974.

Kramer, Lloyd A., and Kramer, Martha B., "The College Library and the Dropout," *College and Research Libraries*, 29:310-312, July, 1968.

Kuehn, J. L., "The Student Drug User and His Family," *Journal of College Student Personnel*, 11:409-413, November, 1970.

Laird, A. W., "Dropout: Analysis of High Aptitude College Students—Western Kentucky's Search for Clues to this Problem," *Western Kentucky Faculty Research Bulletin*, 1:94-98, January, 1969.

Landis, Paul Henry, "A Personal Inventory," pp. 9-22, in *So This Is College*, McGraw-Hill, Book Company, New York, 1954, 205 pp.

Landrith, Harold F., "Two-Year Colleges: Prescription for Junior College Dropouts," *School and Society*, 49:49-51, January, 1971.

Langlois, Eleanor, *Graduate Attrition At Berkeley*, ERIC, no. 699 220, Office of Institutional Research, California University, Berkeley, August, 1972, 59 pp.

Lehmann, Irvin J., "American College Students and the Socialization Process," pp. 58-77, in *The College Student*, edited by Wilbur B. Brookover, The Library of Education, The Center for Applied Research in Education, Inc., New York, 1965, 118 pp.

Less Time More Options—Education Beyond the High School, A special report by the Carnegie Commission on Higher Education, McGraw-Hill Book Company, New York, January, 1971, 45 pp.

Levenson, Edgar A.; Stockhamer, Nathan, and Feiner, Arthur H., "Family Transaction In The Etiology Of Dropping Out of School," *Contemporary Psychoanalysis*, 3:134-157, February, 1977.

Lindsay, Carl A.; Marks, Edmond, and Hamel, Lester S., "Native and Transfer Baccalaureate Students," *The Journal of College Student Personnel*, 7:5-13, January, 1966.

Machlup, Fritz, "Longer Education, Thinner, Broader, or Higher," *A G B Reports*, 14:8-13, September, 1971.

Marks, Edmond, "Student Perceptions of College Persistence and Their Intellective, Personality and Performance Correlates," *Journal of Educational Psychology*, 58:210-221, August, 1967.

Medsker, Leland L., and Trent, James W., "Factors Related To Type of College Attended," pp. 41-50, in *College and Student*, editor, Kenneth A. Feldman, Pergamon Press Inc., New York, 1972, 492 pp.

Meyerson, Martin, "The Ethos of the American College Student: Beyond the Protests," pp. 266-291, in *The Contemporary University*, edited by Robert S. Morrison, Houghton Mifflin, Boston, 1966, 364 pp.

Miser, Kenneth M., *The Impact Of The First Semester Of College On Student Perceptions Of The College Environment And Its Relationship To Academic Achievement And Personal Development*, Unpublished doctor's thesis, School of Education, Indiana University, Bloomington, June, 1971, 207 pp.

Mouly, George J., *The Science of Educational Research*, second edition, Van Nostrand Reinhold Company, New York, New York, 1970, 541 pp.

National Scholarship Service and Fund For Negro Students, *A National Profile of Black Youth, Class of 1971*, ERIC, no. ED 066 120, New York, New York, January, 1972, 115 pp.

Nicholi, Armand M., *An Investigation of Harvard Dropouts*, Final Report, ERIC, no. ED 042 068, Department of Health, Education and Welfare, Washington, D.C., June, 1970, 75 pp.

Pace, Robert C., and Stern, George B., "An Approach To The

Measurement of Psychological Characteristics of College Environments," *Journal of Educational Psychology*, 49:269-277, October, 1958.

Panos, Robert J., and Astin, Alexander W., "Attrition Among College Students," *American Educational Research Journal*, 5:57-72, January, 1968.

Penny, James F., "Student Personnel Work: A Profession Stillborn," *Personnel and Guidance Journal*, 47:958-962, June, 1969.

Pervin, Lawrence A.; Reik, Louis E., and Dalrymple, Willard, pp. 3-21, "The Dropout In Conflict With Society," in *The College Dropout And The Utilization Of Talent*, edited by Lawrence A. Pervin, *et. al.*, Princeton University Press, Princeton, New Jersey, 1966, 260 pp.

Pervin, Lawrence A., *Dissatisfaction With College And The College Dropout: A Transactional Approach*, ERIC, no. ED 021 335, Final Report, Bureau of Research, Office of Education, United States Department of Health, Education and Welfare, Washington, D.C., August, 1967, 47 pp.

Reik, Louis E., M.D., "The College Dropout in Clinical Perspective," pp. 177-187, in *The College Dropout And The Utilization of Talent*, edited by Lawrence A. Pervin, *et. al.*, Princeton University Press, Princeton, New Jersey, 1966, 260 pp.

Richling, John, "70 Per Cent," *Universities Quarterly*, 25:135-138, Spring, 1971.

Ridlon, Howard G., "Why Freshmen Fail," pp. 12-20, in *Introduction To College Life*, by Norman T. Bell, Houghton Mifflin Company, Boston, 1966, 142 pp.

Rivlin, Harry N.; Frazer, Dorothy M., and Stern, Milton R., editors, *The First Years In College: Preparing Students For A Successful College Career*, Little Brown and Company, Boston, 1965, 605 pp.

Robin, Burton and Johnson, Philip, "Identifying Potential Dropouts With Class Lists," *Improving College and University Teaching*, 17:178-179, Summer, 1969.

Robinson, L. F., *Relation Of Student Persistence In College To Satisfaction With "Environmental" Factors*, Unpublished doctor's thesis, University of Illinois, University Microfilms, No. 67-12, 154, Ann Arbor, Michigan, 1967.

Roid, G. H., *Training Self-Management and Study Habits in College Students*, Research Grant Final Report, Center for Learning and Development, McGill University, Quebec, Canada, 1971-72, 27 pp.

Rose, Harriett A., and Elton, Charles, F., "Another Look At The College Dropout," *Journal of Counseling Psychology*, 13:242-245, Summer, 1966.

Rose, Harriett A., and Elton, Charles F., "Attrition and the Vocationally Undecided Student," *Journal of Vocational Behavior*, 1:99-103, January, 1971.

Rossman, Jack E., and Kirk, Barbara A., "Factors Related to Persistence and Withdrawal Among University Students," *Journal of Counseling Psychology*, 17:56-62, January, 1970.

Ryle, Anthony, "Student Health and Student Wastage," *Universities Quarterly*, 25:162-168, Spring, 1971.

Sandell, Sandra A., and Rossman, Jack E., "College Freshmen View Their Parents," *Personnel and Guidance Journal*, 49:821-826, June, 1971.

Saranoff, Irving and Theophile, Raphael, "Five Failing College Students," pp. 289-328, in *Underachievement*, by Milton Kornrich, Charles C. Thomas, Publisher, Springfield, Illinois, 1965, 670 pp.

Savicki, Victor; Schumer, Harry, and Stanfield, Robert E., "Student Role Orientations And College Dropouts," *Journal of Counseling Psychology*, 17:559-566, June, 1970.

Schein, Leon A., "Institutional Characteristics and Student Attitudes," *College Student Survey*, 3:67-69, Winter, 1969.

Schoonmaker, Alan N., "The Freshman Year," pp. 103-113, in *A Student's Survival Manual*, Harper and Row Publishers, New York, New York, 1971, 373 pp.

Schreiber, Daniel, "700,000 Dropouts," *American Education*, 4:5-7, June, 1968.

Shannon, John R., "Percentages of Returns of Questionnaires In Reputable Educational Research," *Journal of Educational Research*, 42:138-141, October, 1948.

Shirey, Warren W., "*Fieldhouse Enrollments 1973-74,*" Interdepartmental Communication, Office of Records and Admissions, Indiana University, Bloomington, August 27, 1973, 2 pp.

Skager, Rodney and others, *Changes In Self-Ratings and Life Goals Among Students At Colleges With Different Characteristics*, ERIC, no. ED 014 095, American College Testing Program, Iowa City, Iowa, August, 1966, 30 pp.

Smith, John Stephen, "A Multivariate Combination of Academic and Non-Academic Factors Related to Student Attrition," *Dissertation Abstracts International*, The Humanities and Social Sciences, 32:6786-A, June, 1972.

Spady, William G., "Dropouts from Higher Education: An Interdisciplinary Review and Synthesis," *Interchange*, 1:64-85, April, 1970.

Starr, Ann; Betz, Ellen L., and Menne, John, "Differences In College Student Satisfaction: Academic Dropouts, Nonacademic Dropouts, And Nondropouts," *Journal of Counseling Psychology*, 19:318-322, July, 1972.

Steedly, Gary F., *Differences In Perception And Academic Achievement Of Superior Students In Relation To Their Living Arrangements*," Unpublished doctor's thesis, School of Education, Indiana University, Bloomington, June, 1971, 94 pp.

Stordahl, Kenneth E., *Influences On College Choice*, ERIC, no. ED 031 143, Institutional Research Office, United States

Department of Health, Education and Welfare, Office of Education, April, 1968, 22 pp.

Sturtz, Sue Anne, "Age Difference in College Student Satisfaction," *The Journal of College Student Personnel*, 12:220-222, May, 1971.

Suczek, Robert and Alfert, Elizabeth, *Personality Development In Two Different Educational Atmospheres*, ERIC, no. ED 042 074, University of California, Berkeley, California, August, 1970, 137 pp.

Suczek, Robert and Alfert, Elizabeth, *Personality Characteristics of College Dropouts*, University of California, Berkeley, California, 1966, 4 pp. mim.

Taylor, Ronald G., and Hanson, Gary R., "Environmental Impact on Achievement and Study Habits," *The Journal of College Student Personnel*, 12:445-454, November, 1971.

Thayer, Robert E., *Do Low Grades Cause College Students To Give Up*, ERIC, no. ED 054 725, Annual Meeting of the Eastern Psychological Association, San Francisco, April, 1971, 5 pp.

Thistlethwaite, Donald L., "College Press and Student Achievement," *Journal of Educational Psychology*, 50:183-191, October, 1959.

Tournoux, J. R., *Le Mois De Mai Du General*, Librarie Plon, Paris, 1969, 527 pp.

Trent, James W., and Medsker, Leland L., *Beyond High School: A Study of 10,000 High School Graduates*, ERIC, no. ED 031 739, Center for Research on Development in Higher Education, Berkeley, California, 1968, 333 pp.

Turner, Hugh J., *The Half That Leaves: A Limited Survey of Attrition In Community Colleges*, ERIC, no. ED 038 127, Florida Community Junior College, Florida University, Gainesville, Florida, March, 1970, 18 pp.

Vaizey, John, "The Costs of Wastage," *Universities Quarterly*, 25:139-145, Spring, 1971.

Vaughan, Richard P., "College Dropouts: Dismissed vs.

Withdrew," *Personnel and Guidance Journal*, 46:685-689, March, 1968.

Vener, Arthur M., "College Education and Vocational Career," pp. 100-116, in *The College Student*, by Wilbur B. Brookover, *et. al.*, The Library of Education, Center for Applied Research in Education, Inc., New York, 1965, 118 pp.

Watley, Donivan J., *Black And Nonblack Youth: Finances And College Attendance*, ERIC, no. ED 082 713, National Merit Scholarship Corporation, Evanston, Illinois, 1971, 21 pp.

Wegner, Eldon L., and Sewell, William H., "Selection and Context As Factors Affecting The Probability of Graduation From College," *American Journal of Sociology*, 75:665-679, January, 1970.

Withey, Stephen B., *A Degree and What Else?*, McGraw-Hill Book Company, New York, New York, 1971, 112 pp.

Yuker, H. E., *et. al.*, *Who Leaves Hofstra For What Reasons*, ERIC, no. ED 065 045, Center for the Study of Higher Education, Hofstra University, Hempstead, New York, May, 1972, 18 pp.

Zaccaria, Lucy and Creaser, James, "Factors Related to Persistence in an Urban Commuter University," *The Journal of College Student Personnel*, 12:286-291, July, 1971.

Appendix: A

DEFINITION OF TERMS

The following terms are defined as indicated for purposes of this research.

Persisting student. A student at any level (freshman, sophomore, junior, senior or graduate) who was enrolled at the major Midwestern university where the research was undertaken at the beginning of the fall, 1973 semester as a full-time student and completed the semester with at least a 2.00 grade point average.

Nonpersisting student. A former student (freshman, sophomore, junior, senior or graduate) who enrolled at this university at the beginning of the fall, 1973 semester and withdrew from school prior to the completion of that semester.

Home environment. The size of the student's family, parent's education levels, and diverse home pressures, such as family health problems, divorce and death.

College environment. The student's relationship with his peers, advisors, faculty members and the student personnel service workers.

Personal characteristics. As indicated by the student's selection of the specific points on the scale (#1=never or seldom, #2=sometimes, or#3=most of the time or always). Bi-polar adjectives will be used to describe the scales continuum of being: happy-unhappy, encouraged-discouraged, healthy-unhealthy, interested-disinterested, certain of his goals-uncertain about his goals, self-confident—lacking self-confidence, satisfactory-unsatisfactory study habits, and adequate high school preparation-inadequate preparation in high school, etc.

College. This term will be used interchangeably with the terms school, university or an institution of higher education.

Appendix: B

SAMPLE OF QUESTIONNAIRE

College Satisfaction Questionnaire

Directions: Please answer each question as you feel it would have applied to you while you were attending the university during the 1973 fall semester.

I. Fill in or check the response most accurate for you.

1. Number of brothers and sisters in your family?
2. Were either of your parents separated (divorced)—yes, —no, or —not living?
3-4. What were the highest grades or degree completed by your parents? Father ——— Mother ———
5. Upon entering college, plans about your educational program were? —certain & decided upon, —partially known, —uncertain & undecided

II. Describe yourself as you feel you were while at the university. Circle #1, 2, or 3.

#1=never or seldom, #2=sometimes, #3=most of the time or always

6. Lacked basic academic skills? 1 2 3
7. Participated in class discussions? 1 2 3
8. Used poor study habits? 1 2 3
9. Interested in school work? 1 2 3

10. Attended classes? 1 2 3
11. Became discouraged? 1 2 3
12. Happy in college? 1 2 3
13. Felt timid or shy? 1 2 3
14. Resented authority? 1 2 3
15. Lacked self confidence? 1 2 3

16. Experienced social problems? 1 2 3
17. Got along with other students? 1 2 3
18. Were you satisfied with the general atmosphere at school? 1 2 3
19. Were you satisfied with your living conditions? 1 2 3
20. Had problems and pressures from parents? 1 2 3

21. Problems at home were:
    —financial
    —health or medical
    —personal
    —none or other (briefly identify)———
    ————————————

22. (Check) Did you drink alcoholic beverages?
    —never
    —once or twice during the semester

—at least once or twice a month
—at least once or twice a week or more frequently

23. Did you use any nonprescription drugs (LSD, marijuana, etc.)?
    —never
    —once or twice during the semester
    —once or twice a month
    —once or twice a week

24. Used the library?
    1=never, or once or twice during the semester
    2=about once or twice a month
    3=about 2 hours per week or more frequently

III. Below are some purposes of higher education. How frequently did you feel these purposes were practiced at the university?

#1=never or seldom, #2=sometimes, #3=most of the time or always

25. To help us grow and develop as human beings. 1 2 3
26. To help us develop independence (be self-sufficient). 1 2 3
27. To help us become more spontaneous and expressive. 1 2 3
28. To help us become more creative (broaden our interests). 1 2 3

29. To help us develop intelligent career plans. 1 2 3
30. To help us develop a sense of trust. 1 2 3
31. To help us become a well rounded person. 1 2 3
32. To help us develop a greater capacity for friendlier relationships with others. 1 2 3

33. To help us become psychologically more healthy. 1 2 3
34. To help us become and feel more important. 1 2 3

35. To help us develop better judgment and wisdom. 1 2 3
36. To help us to learn as much as possible about an academic subject area. 1 2 3
37. Did you ever find a need or reason to talk with or discuss some problem with your academic adviser? —yes, —no
38. If yes, please evaluate his attitude toward you. Circle one of the following numbers: 1 unconcerned, 2 slightly concerned, or 3 concerned.
39. Did you ever find a need or reason to talk with or discuss some problem with any of your faculty members or instructors? —yes, —no
40. If yes, please evaluate their attitude toward you. 1 unconcerned, 2 slightly concerned, or 3 concerned

IV. Please evaluate *only* the student services that you used or came in contact with while at the university. Then evaluate how these services met your needs or helped you with your problem. Circle one number for each service used.

#1=below average, #2=average, or #3=above average

41. Academic Advising 1 2 3
42. Counseling & Psychological Service Center 1 2 3
43. Dean of Students Office 1 2 3
44. Halls of Residence 1 2 3
45. Placement Office 1 2 3
46. University Division Office 1 2 3

47. Reading & Study Skills Center 1 2 3
48. Registrar's Office 1 2 3
49. Student Health Center 1 2 3
50. Scholarship & Financial Aids 1 2 3
51. If any other service or office, please name ─────────────── 1 2 3

V. Were there any specific reasons that made you decide not to continue your education at the university? Please check any items that may apply to you.

52. —financial difficulties
   —marriage
   —health problems
   —failure to make good grades
   —decided on career not requiring college education
   —disliked certain teachers
   —joined U. S. Armed Services
   —had problems with other students
   —became dissatisfied with the general atmosphere & environment at school
   —other reason (please identify)———
   ——————————————

53. Transferred to another college? —yes, —no
54. If yes, transferred because:
   —less expensive at another school
   —wanted a school closer to home
   —other reason (please identify)———
   ——————————————